I ONCE MET
Encounters with the
Famous and Infamous

I ONCE MET

Encounters with the
Famous and Infamous

From the pages of *The Oldie*

With an introduction by Richard Ingrams

OLDIE PUBLICATIONS

First published in 2008
by Oldie Publications Ltd
65 Newman Street, London W1T 3EG
www.theoldie.co.uk

Copyright © Oldie Publications, 2008

ISBN-10: 0954817664
ISBN-13: 978-0954817664

A catalogue record for this book
is available from the British Library

Typeset in 10/13pt Garamond Premier Pro
Printed by CPI Cox & Wyman

Contents

Introduction

IT WAS THE LATE James Michie who had the idea of 'I Once Met'. James, who for a short time was *The Oldie*'s literary editor, supplied the first example – an account of how when he was working as a publisher, he had been sent to help Charlie Chaplin write his memoirs.

James was convinced that once the ball had been set rolling others would follow. And he was perfectly right. Fifteen years later the contributions keep coming in.

Readers of this collection will come across some famous names among the contributors – John Mortimer, A N Wilson, George Mac-Donald Fraser – but the majority of the pieces are supplied by those whom I would describe, for want of a better word, as punters.

The reason why their contributions are generally more interesting is that the great and the good tend to be on their best behaviour when confronted by the professional journalist or interviewer. The stranger, the innocent-looking bystander, has the advantage of observing someone off their guard and perhaps giving themselves away. Would it have occurred to the famous novelist Anthony Powell that the plumber who called at his door one day would write about the meeting and have his piece printed in *The Oldie*? Would E M Forster have refrained from shouting rudely at the young mother wheeling her baby through King's College grounds? Such anecdotes can often give you a more vivid picture than a lengthy biography.

You may notice, along the way, how well written these articles are, further proof that the amateurs can be as good if not better then their professional rivals. My thanks to all of those who have contributed, along with the hope that others may be encouraged to follow their example.

Richard Ingrams, June 2008

Anthony Powell

I AM A plumber who seems to spend most of his time in winter attending to emergency calls, fixing burst pipes, leaks etc. Once, on a freezing January day, I took a call to attend a customer by the name of Powell who had a burst pipe.

I was given directions to the house, which was on the edge of a small village some miles away. After much searching, I eventually drove into the courtyard of what I was almost sure was the right place. I rang the doorbell. An elderly man opened the door and looked at me quizzically. 'Yes,' he said. 'How can I help you?'

'Hello,' I smiled, thinking that my overalls, the toolbox in my hand and my van behind me complete with copper pipes on the roof would make my quest obvious. 'Well?' he said.

'Mr Powell?' I asked. (I pronounced the name 'Pow-well'.) 'There is no one here of that name,' he intoned. 'Oh! Sorry,' I said. 'I must be at the wrong house.' He looked down at me from the step, turned and went back into the house. 'I can't help you,' he said as he shut the door on me.

I drove around in the snow and ice for the next 20 minutes or so, and eventually stopped at the house next to the one I had just called at. The lady living there told me that a gentleman called Anthony Powell did indeed live next door. I went back to the original address and rang the doorbell again. The same man opened the door. This time I tried a different tack. 'Does a Mr Powell live here?' 'No,' he said. 'However, do you mean Pole?' I nodded. 'Ah! Then go round to the back door, the leak is in the kitchen.'

Nigel Day

L S Lowry

I CALLED, unannounced, at the house of L S Lowry when I was aged 12, and he was – what? – 70-odd. 'Bob a job? No thanks. You want what?' I was holding a small portfolio of paintings and drawings to show him. 'You want to be a painter? Better come in.'

Outside, the house was coal-black. Inside was chaos. A back room, from whose ceiling a bare 100-watt bulb dangled, served as a studio. Canvases were leaning everywhere. Paint dribbled down the edge of the easel. The floor was strewn with tubes of more-or-less empty flake white.

'What do you want to know?'

Having been bold enough to visit the famous artist, I did not have the courage to follow it up with any interesting questions. He resumed work on a painting. It was a seascape – streaks of white and grey. No figures, almost no colour, just mist. 'I go more and more to Sunderland. I like the sea. And I'll let you into a secret about why I like painting either houses and streets or the sea. I can't draw trees at all. Never could. Another reason I go to the seaside so much these days is that I hate this house. Always have done. An absolutely horrible house.' For a while he daubed in silence. I asked an idiot schoolboy question – 'I wonder how many tubes of white paint you have got through in the course of your life?'

'Now, if you become a painter, you won't find it easy to make money.

By no means!'

His face came very close to mine. I was struck by his prison pallor, and the very bright blue eyes and by the white hair *en brosse*, like a polar bear's.

Insensitively, I hung around for hours. He made me tea. Then he went and changed from his paint-spattered suit into a clean one, and placed a hat on his head – a trilby whose crown he had carefully punched out to make it the shape of a bowler.

He told me that he would escort me back to Manchester, presumably the only way he could think of getting rid of me.

'Thank you, sir' – this to the bus conductor who gave us our tickets. Then, to me, 'Do you enjoy music? Which composers?' I said Schubert. 'Well, you could do much worse than Schubert. I like to listen to the gramophone while I'm working. Now the difference between an artist and everyone else is that everyone else is only happy when they stop working. An artist is only happy when he is working. But oh, it does make me tired. Do you see that wall? I once saw a man lying on top of that wall. I did a painting of it. Oh yes, I'm tired. Want to go back to the seaside.'

Mr Lowry had spent the better part of a day with me, and delivered me to my mother, who was having tea in one of the larger department stores – Marshall and Snelgrove, I think. When he had gone, I realised that I had left my small portfolio of paintings and drawings behind at his house. I would never have dared to go back for them.

A N Wilson

Bobby Fischer

IT WAS MY first assignment as a reporter on *Life* magazine and I was nervous. When the photographer, Doug Rodewald, arrived, he was puffing slightly under the weight of his equipment. He put it down between us like a challenge. I'd been told that a reporter should never help carry a photographer's equipment; it established the wrong relationship. But he was at least 10 years older than me and 40 pounds heavier. I picked up his tripod and a small box and told myself that I'd toughen up as I got more experienced. We drove off to Brooklyn to do a story on a 12-year-old chess prodigy.

At the time Bobby Fischer was in the fourth grade of his local high school and regularly beating the best adult players in the country. He lived at home with his mother and I had to convince her that a story in *Life* could help her son's career without spoiling his character. Their apartment was on the first floor of a clapperboard house in a poor but still respectable part of Brooklyn. Bobby Fischer was tall and gangling, but with a physique that looked certain to fill out in a couple of years. Taciturn when I first met him, he was even more taciturn when introduced to Doug Rodewald. His mother, Mary, was around 40 and worked as a nurse. She was a tough-looking lady. Initially there had been no mention of Bobby's father. I had to screw up a lot of courage to get her into the kitchen and ask who and where the father was. She didn't want him mentioned in the story. Readers, I said, would at least want to know who he was. If we didn't mention it at all it would attract even more curiosity. Naturally we would mention it very discreetly. She said quickly that she and Bobby's father divorced over ten years before. That was it. The subject was closed. All this was said in a low whisper. His father was clearly not a topic she ever discussed with – or in front of – Bobby, let alone in front of a *Life* reporter and photographer.

The bleak, under-furnished apartment was obviously not inspiring Doug Rodewald to flights of photographic fancy. He tried engaging Bobby and failed. 'Great picture story this is going to be,' he hissed at me. I knew that the secret of photo-journalism in a static situation was that the subject must become aware of the camera. Either this was achieved by the photographer clicking off so many pictures that the subject forgot he was there, or by the subject being distracted by the reporter's penetrating questions. Asking Bobby Fischer questions proved a thankless task. He gave monosyllabic answers and then glanced irritably at the camera.

His mother was sensitive enough to realise my predicament. She took me aside – 'Do you play chess?'

I told her I hadn't played for about four years and hadn't been very good, even then.

'Try,' she said. 'It's the only way you'll get him to relax.'

There was no alternative. For the success of my first assignment I would offer myself as sacrificial lamb to this disgruntled 12-year-old.

'How about a game of chess?'

He looked at me with mild interest for the first time.

'You any good?'

'Bit rusty, but I wasn't too bad.' If I could hold him at bay for even half-a-dozen moves, Rodewald might get a few relaxed pictures.

'They're beautiful,' I said, as Bobby Fischer laid out a set of finely carved ivory pieces.

'I won them. You can be white.'

I remembered an opening I had used effectively at college. I made my moves very slowly. His moves came like lightning. For about four moves I felt I was holding my own and then I realised he was going to make a total monkey out of me. I was walking straight into one of the oldest traps in the game. Rodewald was taking his pictures infuriatingly slowly, and I was going to be demolished in minutes. I had to hang on at least for a few more moves.

Then suddenly, a miracle – a glowing light shone round my queen's bishop, illuminating its path to king's knight 5; the way out of the trap. If only! I decided to sacrifice my knight, but he didn't take it. He had a smarter plan. A few moves later it was checkmate.

'You shouldn't have moved your knight,' was all he said.

'Beaten already?' Rodewald said, but he looked happy. He had his pictures.

Two days later we went to the prestigious Manhattan Chess Club and took pictures of Bobby Fischer beating a grandmaster. There were only about half-a-dozen of them in the US. The Club secretary assured me that one day, sooner rather than later, Bobby Fischer would be the first American World Champion.

Two years later Bobby Fischer became US chess champion. A year later he became an international grandmaster and qualified to challenge for the world championship. In 1972 in Reykjavik, at the age of 26, he became world chess champion. Even before that he had been highly unpredictable and demanding. He soon became even stranger, and didn't play chess in public for another 20 years. In 1992, when Serbia was under American sanctions, Fischer defied his government and played Spassky in Belgrade. His passport was revoked and he was regarded as a traitor. He became wildly anti-semitic and welcomed the 9/11 attack on New York. He was imprisoned in Japan while he awaited extradition to the US. Now he has been saved by Iceland. I hope he will be happy there and even start playing chess again. I doubt if I will. I haven't played since I lost to him.

Stanley Price

Evelyn Waugh

EVELYN WAUGH was at his eccentric best in 1953 when we arrived to record an interview for Far Eastern listeners at Pier's Court in Stinchcombe, known to friends as 'Stinkers', its brass plate announcing 'No Admittance on Business'. As the recording cable was run into the house he expressed great concern that his wife's cows, chewing the cud in a field a hundred yards away, should not be electrocuted by accident. After some confusion the interview began. He chose to sit behind his desk in the library, wearing a grey suit, waistcoat, watch-chain and a Brigade of Guards tie. 'My original ambition was to become a painter and after that a carpenter,' he declared. 'But I found that I was too lazy to acquire very much facility in either of these crafts, while my whole education had gone to make me literary.'

Drink had been his main interest at university. 'I took a bad Third.' All music was painful to him, with the possible exception of plainchant. Decent architecture ceased about the time he was born.

This visit preceded publication of *The Ordeal of Gilbert Pinfold*, a name borrowed from an earlier owner of Pier's Court. Pinfold was harassed by the voice of a BBC interviewer. So why did Waugh agree in 1960 to go on television in *Face to Face*? He requested a ridiculously large fee and a contract was devised including every conceivable right. He accepted. Had he agreed the original offer the total would have been greatly increased by repeat fees.

I went with Felix Topolski for lunch to Combe Florey, near Taunton, a house without a television set and a radio only in the servants' quarters. He pretended to be surprised that we had not arrived, as gentlemen normally did, by train. Over lunch he asked what would be required of him. 'Will the studio be very hot? Would I need to wear my tropical clothes?' I assured him that the black drapes of the set would keep him cool. 'You mean I'll be given one to wear?' When the time came for Topolski to start sketching, Waugh was aghast. 'But where's your easel, Mr Topolski? What! You don't use an easel?' As Felix sketched, Waugh discussed, among many things, buggery on Mount Athos. Then it was time for afternoon tea. As we got up I admired the chandelier. 'That's not a chandelier – that's a gasolier! Are you interested in gasoliers?' and off I was taken to admire the gasoliers. We arrived in the dining-room where a large tureen of green-tufted strawberries was waiting. Too late I saw the problem. Put the strawberries on the plate, add the cream, take the spoon – and you were trapped with the strawberry tufts. My attempt to spear one shot it under the sideboard. That was the BBC disgraced. Topolski, seeing what had happened, did the socially unthinkable – dipped a strawberry into the cream with his fingers. 'Ah, Mr Topolski,' Waugh observed helpfully, 'you need a spoon.'

When he arrived at Lime Grove it became clear that his illness had not completely evaporated. 'Where's the hidden microphone?' he enquired. His eyes settled on the wire of the electric clock. 'Ah yes. I see.' When John Freeman arrived I introduced them. Waugh stepped back, horrified. 'The name is Waugh – not Wuff!' he protested. 'But I called you Mr Waugh,' Freeman smiled. 'No, no, I distinctly heard you say "Wuff",' continued the great writer, lighting a cigar. I read later that he had checked for any defamatory information about his interviewer in case he needed it for defence or offence.

When asked why he was appearing on television he replied: 'Poverty. We are both being hired to talk in this deliriously happy way.' Freeman challenged him on this pose of poverty. Waugh replied: 'Never saved a penny. And of course no honest man has been able to save any money in the last 20 years.' His worst fault was irritability. With? 'Absolutely everything. Inanimate objects and people, animals, anything.'

The game continued after the filming. A postcard, addressed to 'The Director General of *Face to Face*', said he had found a cigar-cutter in his pocket which was not his. Was it mine? I replied that I was not missing a cigar-cutter. Another card arrived after the film was transmitted. 'Thank you for your letter. I did not see the exhibition but somebody who did remarked that it seemed to end abruptly. I assure you I don't care. E W, SS Peter & Paul 1960.' The transmission had indeed ended abruptly. John Freeman had asked as a closing question whether, looking back on the mental breakdown, he could see a conflict between the way he had been brought up and the lifestyle he had chosen to live. 'Oh, I know what you're getting at. That ass Priestley said that in an article... Poor old Priestley thought that.' BBC lawyers decided the reference might take us all into court, so it was chopped off. A pity because *Priestley v Waugh* on whether Priestley was an ass would have been worth every penny of a legal action.

Hugh Burnett

Harpo Marx

I WAS ON *Picture Post* at the time, editing the so-called funny page, or rather, preparing specimen funny pages to show what they could be like. I had at my disposal any number of artists and writers to help me, including Patrick Campbell, then on the staff of *Lilliput* (like *Picture Post*, one of the Hulton group). Harpo Marx was in London, making a personal appearance at the Palace Theatre in a variety show. He appeared, dressed as usual in his shaggy wig of red hair and capacious, shapeless garments straight from a rag-bag. He played his harp: serious music, beautifully performed. We all applauded loudly; Harpo came forward to the front of the stage to acknowledge the applause. He bowed, and as he did so a spoon dropped out of a sleeve. He looked embarrassed. A couple more dropped from the other sleeve, and then more. Spoons and knives and forks, clattering in a cascade from his garments, each offering making him more and more embarrassed. It was astounding. He stood ankle-deep in the things. How on earth he had played the harp, and so well, for so long, while carrying such a weight of cutlery no-one will ever know. It was incredibly, earth-shakingly funny.

We cut here to Harpo's bedroom at the Savoy. (I was a bit disappointed at the ordinariness of a Savoy bedroom). How I got there is as mysterious as the spoons and forks disgorged by Harpo on the Palace Theatre stage. I had recently been to the National Gallery and had noticed the astonished likeness of one of the figures in a Rubens painting to Harpo. When shown a photograph of the painting, Harpo agreed. In real life, small, bald and very Jewish, he was a man you wouldn't notice on a bus or in a supermarket. He was wearing an open-necked shirt and ordinary trousers. At once he put on the magic wig. Somehow his eyes popped. He tucked the collar of his shirt inside and used his two little fingers to make the double pan-pipes of Bacchus's attendant. The photographs were taken. I thanked him, no doubt profusely, and we left.

Harpo Marx was the chap in the picture, as I had hoped, though fittingly, not a word of what he said, being who he was, has stayed in my memory.

Selwyn Powell

Philip Larkin

IN 1928 I was a six-year-old pupil at Cheshunt School, Manor Road, Coventry. This was a preparatory school for girls but also accepted boys at kindergarten level. The school was a converted suburban house with ample garden and extra classrooms built on, and was owned and run by the Miss Bottomleys (Miss Ethel and Miss Evelyn). One day, as I remember it was mid-term, a new boy arrived. Not yet possessing a school uniform, he was conspicuous in a sailor suit and flat sailor hat, complete with ribbon and HMS *Pinafore* in gold letters across the front. This was Philip Larkin. We were the same age, in the same form together, and naturally became friends.

I remember Philip at school entertaining us during morning breaks with stories accompanied by illustrations on the blackboard. These were humorous, often with a strong excremental bias and therefore guaranteed to get a laugh from six-year-old boys. (I recall one vivid drawing of an aircraft crashing into the local sewage works.) On Saturdays we would play football together with other little boys in our road. Philip was a goalkeeper of moderate ability, but was handicapped at ball games by his myopia, which I don't think was then recognised.

Senior oldies will perhaps recall the importance of cigarette-card collecting to schoolboys in the period between the wars. Most fathers and uncles smoked Players Navy Cut or Wills Goldflake. There was little to choose between the two brands, and I would encourage my father to alternate according to which set of cards I happened to be collecting. The competition to be the first in the school with a complete set was intense, especially if footballers or cricketers were the subject of the series.

In late 1929 or early 1930 a new series of cards was issued consisting of international rugby footballers. I had collected about half the set and kept the cards in an album specially designed for them. One day when I was about to add new cards to my collection, I discovered that at least half were missing. I was distraught and let out a bellow of tearful rage, alerting the rest of the family to the situation. Circumstantial evidence pointed to Philip as prime suspect. My mother was emphatic: he had been looking through the album only recently when on a lunchtime visit.

How to obtain proof or, more importantly, retrieve the cards was another matter. The family were sympathetic but perhaps did not appreciate the full magnitude of my loss. My best friend Peter, who was also collect-ing the series, was more understanding. He was nearly a year older and, at the age of eight and a half, capable of righteous indignation. He over-came my diffidence and together we called at the Larkin house, accusing Philip of taking the cards, and demanding them back. He did return them. Unfortunately they had been defaced: all the beautiful red, white, blue and green shirts had been obliterated beneath a pattern of fine cross-hatching in blue-black ink! Decades later, in memorable English, Philip laid much blame on his mum and dad. I wouldn't know about that; but certainly in terms of f***ing things up, he did a Grade A job on my cigarette cards.

Glyn Lloyd

The Red Dean

EASTER 1954. My wife and I were recently married. We thought that a quick visit to the ancient town of Canterbury might be a fitting excursion. The coach service from London was good, and we were soon strolling in the hallowed precincts of the famous Cathedral, enjoying the early spring weather.

The first surprise was to see alongside the Deanery a group of sinister-looking, muscle-bound heavies, their armpits bulging with very obvious revolver holsters. A cluster of heavily reinforced foreign cars completed the ensemble. As we looked more closely, they glared back aggressively. It was clearly a case for walking on.

We entered the main door of the Cathedral. There was a sudden commotion. Some of the few other visitors present climbed on chairs and pews. It all looked very unseemly. Right before us, a few yards away, stood the Red Dean himself, Dr Hewlett Johnson, red-faced, grizzled hair and conspicuously vain. Alongside him was a podgy, grey-faced, drably clothed, slightly bewildered-looking figure. A swathe of greasy black hair cut across his forehead. It was Georgi Malenkov, supposedly the appointed heir to Joseph Stalin, who had died the year before.

For a few seconds, we gazed in awe and silence. Then the Dean stepped forward and trilled in a mellifluous voice: 'I know that you are not showing the gladness of your feelings in these holy surroundings. But I know too that you have a song in your heart at meeting Mr Malenkov.'

With horror, I heard my wife murmur 'Rubbish'.

The Dean glided on, exalted and apparently oblivious to anything else but walking in the presence of the leader of World Communism. Georgi Malenkov looked increasing bemused as the gaitered Dean escorted him out of the house of God. They looked an odd couple indeed.

We never quite got to know whether Mr Malenkov was a force for good or just a repolished figure of the old regime. Before long, he was transported to some outpost in the Soviet Union to eke out his time, powerless and broken.

Peter Shapcott

Jean Louis Barrault

IN 1963 I WAS chief electrician at the Aldwych theatre, which was leased to the Royal Shakespeare Company, who played there from September to June. In the remaining summer months Peter Daubeny presented his World Theatre Season. Compared to the RSC season, this was a doddle. The same show every night for a week, and a ready-made one at that. We still had to work every weekend of course, but that was money in the bank, boozer or betting shop, depending on your inclinations.

The 'Theatre de France' arrived at about midnight on Saturday with a lot of Gallic flap and fluster. The set was erected, the lamps were hung, coloured and focused, and by Monday morning we were ready for the lighting session, which was to be conducted by the director, Monsieur Jean Louis Barrault.

Monsieur Barrault eventually appeared and we duly set to work. Things went well throughout the morning, so we took a short lunch break and then continued in the afternoon.

Theatre directors treat electricians, carpenters and the like in one of two ways. They either ignore you completely for the most part and then say 'I suppose the electricians are all in the pub' when you are standing beside them. Or, worse still, they treat you like some beloved family retainer who is slightly dotty and has to be cajoled into everything. Both types have an irritating mannerism. They say 'Can we?' when they mean

'Will you?' Some of the muttered responses I've heard to 'Can we sweep the stage?' would unnerve a brewer's drayman.

The famous Frenchman was very different. For one thing, he wouldn't stand still. One minute he'd be on stage checking something and the next his voice would come from the back of the upper circle telling us to throw some lamp out of focus because it was making ugly lines on the floor. He kept up a continuous dialogue with his stage management and various administrative people who wandered on and off stage throughout the day. He was a whirlwind of a man who seemed to have tons of time for everyone and everything.

Towards the end of the day things slowed down a lot and I expressed concern that we were running a bit late and that I'd have to break the crew before the performance. He turned to the stage and shouted some rapid French. It had an immediate effect and the proceedings moved on apace. I asked Maggie what he had said. She wasn't sure, so we enquired. 'Ah!' he said. 'It is a very useful expression. What is the word you use meaning to make love to a woman?' Maggie, who had been properly brought up, said, 'Oh dear! I suppose you mean "fuck".'

'Exactly,' he said. 'I told them to stop trying to fuck a fly. You must have a similar expression in English. No?'

Maggie thought for a bit. 'I suppose our closest would be "to split hairs".' We all agreed that '*arretez d'enculer les mouches*' had much more style.

At about 4.30pm Barrault stopped and told me to give the crew a break. I said that as there was very little left to do we may as well finish it. 'No,' he said. 'Tell your men to go home and make babies. We can finish when they come back.' I obviously didn't look too happy about the idea because he gave me some advice. 'On a first night to have nervous actors is a good thing. To have nervous technicians is a disaster.'

I have never forgotten that remark and have had cause to repeat it once or twice when faced with bad directions from men of less talent and wisdom. We finished our work on time. The curtain rose and on came the indefatigable Jean Louis to give a splendid three-hour performance. I don't know if any babies were made.

David A Read

Noël Coward

I ONCE HAD WORDS with Noël Coward. Well, I had several and he had one. I triumphed – or so I thought at the time.

It was in the 1940s while he was on a fund-raising tour of South Africa. He did two nights in Kimberley, where they mine the myth that diamonds are forever.

I was a cub reporter, er, the only reporter, on the *Diamond Fields Advertiser* and donned an ill-fitting hat as theatre critic for the night. I was, predictably, bowled over by Coward's performance and wrote at length and with enthusiasm to that effect. At the same time, I was unimpressed by his accompanist, Lionel Bowman, and said as much, but in fewer words.

The next morning my editor had an irate telephone call from Coward, doubtless with Bowman fuming at his elbow, demanding the most abject apology for my scandalous and utterly unwarranted references to his estimable fellow artist. I was summoned to meet Coward in his dressing room *that very night*. I jumped at this chance of meeting the great man face-to-face and duly presented myself for the dressing down.

He said: 'Well?'

I explained that, with the greatest respect, I could not possibly apologise for writing what I believed, rightly or wrongly, to be true. Bowman's support had been, in my humble view, woefully short of the standard set by his principal. There was a brief silence. Coward offered me a whisky and, without another word, returned to his application of make-up. That was that.

It was only in my more mature years, as editor of the self-same provincial daily, that I came to realise why Coward was happy to let the matter rest where it did.

The reason was that we were all left ever so happy. I thought I had struck a resounding blow for press freedom. Bowman believed my guts had been reduced to garters. Coward ensured the show went on. It did.

Archie Atkinson

Lord Montgomery

FIELD MARSHAL Lord Montgomery of Alamein took an interest in a number of boys' schools after the war. Westminster Abbey Choir School, which I attended from 1949 to 1953, was one. His relationship with the school began in 1947 while he was still Chief of the Imperial General Staff. The Dean and Chapter's efforts to re-establish the Choir School quickly after the war were frustrated by the fact that the building remained in the hands of the War Office. Despite representations at the highest level there seemed little hope of success. Monty had a flat at Westminster, and attended matins at the Abbey. After one such visit, a word in his ear resulted in the building being handed over two weeks later.

So began a long association with the school and its boys. For the Coronation in 1953, his flat having 'gone with the job', Monty and his page lodged with us in Dean's Yard, just behind the Abbey. After one of the final rehearsals, Monty announced that he and his page would pose on the school steps in their full regalia. It was a command rather than an invitation that we should photograph them.

A number of us trooped out dutifully with our Box Brownies.

Press photographers were always lurking about in Dean's Yard at that time, and it was no surprise when, the following day, a pictured appeared in the *Daily Mirror* of us taking photographs of Monty.

After choir practice that morning I was summoned to the Headmaster's office. There stood Monty and his page. The Headmaster addressed me sternly. 'The Field Marshal would like a word with you,' he said.

'Is that you, boy?' said Monty, pointing to the photograph in the *Daily Mirror* (see previous page). 'Yes sir, it is,' I replied. 'And that's Keith Hewitt and...' 'I'm not interested in the others,' he interjected. 'Notice anything about the photograph, eh?' I looked at it carefully. 'No sir, I don't. It's rather a good one of...' 'SOCKS, boy, SOCKS!' he yelled suddenly. The Headmaster's hand shot to his mouth to stifle a giggle. The page, to whom a number of us had taken a distinct dislike, smirked superciliously.

'You've got one sock up and one sock down,' squeaked a furious Monty. 'You're a disgrace, boy! A disgrace to me and the School. Explain yourself.' I was mortified. 'Gosh, sir,' I said, 'I'm dreadfully sorry. I've lost one of my garters, and... I can't explain it, sorry sir.' Monty and the smug-faced page swept out of the room. After more mumbled apologies to the Headmaster, and on the verge of tears, I left the study. I went straight to my copy of the picture and cut off the offending leg. At least my parents would not see my shame when they saw the photograph in my scrapbook, where it remains to this day.

The story might have ended there, but on leaving the Abbey Choir School, I went to St John's School, Leatherhead, where Monty was chairman of the governors. An Abbey chorister was a bit of a novelty after the Coronation, and on my first speech day I was called on to the sacred grass of the quad to shake hands with the great man.

'I know you, boy,' he cried, before I could be introduced. 'You're the boy who can't keep his socks up.' He glared at me ferociously and, before I could say anything, added, 'Things don't seem to have improved.' I looked down. No problem there. Even he couldn't see through long trousers. Shoes looked OK. 'Your JACKET,' he shrieked. 'It's got a button missing!'

David Ransom

Fats Waller

I WAS FIVE years old when I started piano lessons. The Roaring Twenties were just beginning in America, but things were still quite demure where we lived, in Sussex. Nevertheless, by the time the 1930s rolled round I was already in love (via the radio) with the popular songs of the day and knew the names of the most famous singers and jazz musicians across the Atlantic. I had one particular favourite, Fats Waller, and loved the infectious rhythm and personality which poured out of his records. By the age of 15 I was buying every Waller record that came out.

There was great excitement when Fats Waller's tour of Britain was announced in 1938, and I was at Sherry's Club in Brighton to see his single performance. Dozens of people crowded around him at the end; I was too shy to get close. The following year I read in the *Melody Maker* that Fats was scheduled for a return tour. This time I must try to meet him. War was approaching, and I thought, 'It's now or never.' Luckily, an old school-friend worked as the orchestra steward on the *Queen Mary*. On the way over from New York Fats played with a small jazz group drawn from the ship's dance band, and my friend got him to sign some photos for me.

Fats appeared as top-of-the-bill on a variety show at the Brighton Hippodrome for the week starting 8th May 1939. On Thursday night I caught the 7 o'clock bus from Steyning, watched the show from the front of the house and then, armed with the signed photos, went to the stage door to ask whether I could meet the great man. 'Yes, go on down, he'll be pleased to see you,' said the doorman.

Moments later I was showing my hero the photos and explaining that I was the 'Hazel' he'd dedicated them to. Some other people were there and a discussion started about who had actually written 'Deep Purple', a brand new popular song of that year. I shyly said, 'I think it was Peter de Rose.' Fats seemed very impressed, and also with the news that I hoped to return for his Friday and Saturday performances. 'If you do,' he said, 'come straight to the stage door and you can watch me from the wings.'

As he came offstage on the Saturday night he suddenly reached up and swung on a beam above us and shouted, 'Well, how was I?' I said he was wonderful, but when he suddenly said teasingly, 'Hazel, honey, why don't I come over for tea one day and meet your mom?' I became flustered. I had sudden visions of him arriving unannounced and my old grandmother opening our door to this enormous black American entertainer! I was invited to a party after the show, but I had to catch the last bus, and even though I was 22 my mother would have been worrying. Things were different in those days.

The following week a little parcel arrived, posted from the Grand Hotel, Brighton. Fats had enclosed one of his lovely silk ties – brown, with gold musical instruments embossed on it – and also some publicity photos of himself. On one of them he had written: 'To my good girlfriend Hazel – may you always be blessed from above. Your friend, sincerely, Thomas "Fats" Waller.' I still have the tie, and during the war years, when I worked as a welder, I wore it every day under my overalls for good luck.

Hazel Mundell

Albert Pierrepoint

AS A NATIONAL Serviceman, I was posted to the 5 Field Squadron Workshops Royal Engineers in Hameln, West Germany in 1948. One day, I was told to report to Hameln Jail and wait in a small room in the guard house. After ten minutes or so the door opened and in walked a short, stocky man in blue waistcoated suit and trilby hat. 'Hello,' he said, putting out his hand. 'I'm Albert Pierrepoint. I expect you've heard of me.' 'Yes,' I stammered, wondering what on earth I was doing there.

'It's like this,' he said. 'You have to take the coffin away after I've hung him.' 'Hung who?' I asked. 'Oh, a war criminal who was tracked down after the war because he had shot 25 British soldiers who were prisoners of war after making them dig their graves. Would you like to come and see him sent to his Maker?' he asked.

All of this was a bit of a shock for a 19-year-old. I stammered my thanks and he said, 'Fine, I'll come and fetch you.' I sat there, all sorts of things flashing through my mind. Fifteen minutes later he appeared, just the same, trilby hat still on head. He led me to a bleak warehouse, standing in the middle of which was the gallows, rope still in place, and a coffin with a lid being screwed on by a German dressed in fatigues.

Pierrepoint jumped up on to the coffin to hold the lid down while it was being screwed on. 'I like to do that,' he said. 'Don't want him trying to get out!'

With no more ado the coffin was lifted on to my lorry, I was given a map and off I went, with Pierrepoint's last words ringing in my ears: 'See you for dinner tonight in Hameln in the restaurant in the square.' 'OK,' I shouted. What else could I do?

Up in the Harz Mountains I drove to a secret cemetery, manned by old Germans and one British officer. 'You aren't here, are you?' he said. 'No,' I replied. 'You've got the idea,' he said. 'We don't want a lot of old Nazis coming here to worship at these b******s' graves in the future, do we?' 'No,' I said.

The coffin was carried to a prepared grave – I had never realised how deep graves are. There were no ropes, so we held it over the hole and let it drop and it hit the bottom with a tremendous crash. 'Bloody good riddance,' the officer said, and I drove off as quickly as I could.

As good as his word, I met Albert – 'Call me Albert,' he said – that night. He was a very nice chap, who had no conscience about his job. He told me he'd met Winston Churchill, who told him he was carrying out the wishes of the British people and doing a good job. Hanging had been in his family. His father was also the government hangman, and had a pub, The Hangman's Arms, somewhere in the Midlands.

He explained the technicalities of hanging – it was an 'art', he said – but the details are too delicate for *Oldie* readers. He believed he would be the last Government hangman, and he was paid £50 plus expenses for each procedure. He said you had to be totally detached. Most of the time he was certain they were guilty, though he wanted Ruth Ellis reprieved. It was not to be, and he felt this was quite wrong.

So the evening passed – but what sort of conversation could a 19-year-old have with such a man? I did my best. When I wrote to tell my parents, they were appalled!

Some 15 years later I was having a drink with my chairman in his office one evening when he told me he had received a book over Christmas about two soldiers who had been made to dig their own graves with some 20 others, and were then machine-gunned. They had survived, been rescued by the Resistance, nursed back to health and taken back to

England.

Their senior officer did not believe their story and they were almost accused of desertion. They wrote personally to Winston Churchill, who believed them, met them and promised that the man would be hunted down, tried and executed.

'I buried him!' I said.

P L Steer

Lionel Begleiter

ON 10 APRIL 1948, 15 years old and the personification of inexperience, I started my new job as messenger boy and trainee at Zec Limited, the Baker Street commercial art studios founded by Philip Zec, the *Daily Mirror's* political cartoonist.

It would be my job to sweep the floors, wash out and refill the artists' water jars, run for cigarettes, tobacco, Chelsea buns, rubber nails, and buckets of steam, and to deliver parcels of artwork to stylish advertising agencies around the West End. My arrival *ipso facto* promoted the previous boy, who would now show me the ropes and then move on to the drawing board, leaving most of the drudgery to me.

He was a little older and bulkier than I. Olive-skinned beneath a mop of black curly hair, he had a bulbous nose, a thick, cocky, cockney accent, and an East Ender's swagger. He over-awed me, the new boy from the north Surrey suburbs, full of innocence and yet instinctively aware of his street-wisdom which, I somehow knew, might be the saving of me if I could tap into it.

As the weeks went by he showed me how to go by bus and pocket the taxi fare. He revealed the whereabouts of J Walter Thompson, Erwin Wasey or S H Benson, and he fired my youthful lust with his encyclopaedic knowledge of the minds and bodies of their receptionists. He made known the secret ways: the narrow, smelly connecting tunnels and alleys or the fast nip through Brown's Hotel from Albemarle Street to Bond Street. He pointed out the street girls in Lisle Street and Shepherd Market; showed me how to fiddle the Waygood-Otis pre-selector in the housing on the roof of our building to cause the lift to stop between floors so that we could rescue the office girls from the Sta-Blonde Laboratories; and I joined him, with an enormous sense of audacity, pouring Coca-Cola over the barrow boy in the street below the studio after he'd sold us a bag of rotten cherries for sevenpence.

But in a serious vein, perhaps the most important thing he ever did for me was to kill an unquestioned prejudice inherited from my childhood.

One day, walking along New Oxford Street, wanting to show off my grown-uppedness, I nudged him and pointed at a black-clad, Homburg-hatted figure and said: 'Look at that greasy old Jew'.

Lionel stopped me dead. 'Why did you say that?'

'I-I don't know,' I stammered, shocked by the look of anger and hurt on his face.

'Don't you know that I'm a Jew?' he asked.

'No.'

'Look at my skin, my hair, my nose; listen to my voice – my name is Begleiter! What did you think I was?'

The plain fact was that, too young, too wet, I had no idea. 'Italian?' I hazarded, awkwardly.

He shrugged, palms upward, and looked to heaven. Then he laughed and put his arm around my shoulders. 'Think before you speak in future,' he warned.

My unthinking prejudice and his understanding forgiveness are lessons I have never forgotten.

Year later, when I had gone to live abroad, I read an article about the brilliant man who had written the musical *Oliver!* There was his photo-graph. I knew that face. It was Lionel Begleiter.

Excitedly, I wrote to him care of the London theatre which was staging the show. Although it was a long shot, I hoped the letter would find him, for I wanted simply to remind him of our days as messenger boy-commercial art trainees and to congratulate him on his success. Some weeks later a mauve, slightly scented envelope arrived in my mailbox. It contained a mauve, slightly scented letter from his secretary.

'Mr Bart is unable to answer your letter as he is fully engaged in working on his new musical...'

I never did hear from him, in person. I wonder whether he ever did read my letter? I believe his fortunes later fluctuated and I have no idea what happened to him. I'll not forget him, though. He was a good teacher.

Now that he's an oldie he might read this. It's a reminiscence by way of saying 'thank you'.

Don Donovan

Albert Schweitzer

MOST PEOPLE will probably remember the name Albert Schweitzer as the founder for a hospital for lepers at Lambaréné in Gabon, West Africa. He was a missionary surgeon and was awarded the Nobel Peace Prize in 1952. He was also an accomplished musician, an authority on J S Bach , and a widely-travelled organist.

I was in my second year as organ scholar of Keble College, Oxford (1932) when I received a message from John Dykes Bower, fellow and organist of New College, inviting me to assist Dr Schweitzer in his forth-coming recital on the New College chapel organ. Schweitzer apparently always needed two people to pull out the stops. I was to be in charge of stops on Schweitzer's left-hand side and his wife would manage the stops on his right. The height of the organ loft, plus some curtains, shielded us from public view.

The directions for the stops were printed in the score in two colours – red and blue. The red referred to my side and the blue to Madame Schweitzer's. As we came up to a marking Schweitzer would call out 'Yetst' (German *'Jetzt'* meaning 'now') and one of us would act according to the colour.

All seemed to go smoothly for a while until on the call of a 'Yetst', Madame Schweitzer unaccountably pulled out *her* stop despite the fact the writing was red (my side).

Dr Schweitzer cut short his playing and in a loud voice thundered abuse at his poor weeping wife and ordered her out of the organ loft.

I remember being in a state of slight shock and stayed in my corner. Then John Dykes Bower, who had been listening down in the chapel, appeared in the organ loft. Pretending not to notice that anything was amiss, he suggested to Schweitzer that he might like to hear the sound of the organ in the chapel below.

So Schweitzer clambered down the steps and Dykes Bower played. He was a better player than Schweitzer whose playing was efficient rather than inspired and whose tempi were very slow. When Schweitzer returned it was a relief to see that the little diversion had dispelled his black mood. He congratulated Dykes Bower on his playing, Madame Schweitzer was reinstated, and we continued with the rehearsal.

After all these years, I still wonder how Madame Schweitzer made that mistake and why Dr Schweitzer was so terribly angry with her. But I wouldn't have missed the bizarre happenings in New College organ loft for anything.

Joseph Cooper

Robert Graves

I ONCE MET Robert Graves. He was old, I don't know how old, but eternally handsome, grey-haired, and he sat like an emperor on a sofa beside me and said, 'Jesus Christ, of course, lived to the age of 80, when he went to China and discovered spaghetti.' Someone else, so far as I can remember it was Jo Grimond, was also on the sofa with us. Mr Graves had puzzled him. 'Which Gospel is it exactly?' he asked politely, 'in which we read that Jesus went to China and discovered spaghetti?' 'It's not in a Gospel,' Graves answered with imperious simplicity. 'It's a well-known fact of history.'

Later I said, 'We all remember what you did in the 1914 war, but what did you do in the last war?'

'I won the Battle of Anzio.' he told me.

'How did you manage that?'

'Well I was cycling around the island of Jersey during the War and I met an officer in my old regiment, the Welsh Guards. I asked him what he was doing and he said, 'We're off to fight the Eyeties.' So I said, 'I'll think of a plan by which you can beat the Eyeties.' So I cycled round the island again and when I got back to him I said, 'There's one thing that really scares an Eyetie and that is the cry of a woman in labour. So you want to go to Queen Charlotte's Hospital and record all the women in labour, then play their cries on gramophones to the Eyeties and they'll run a mile.' Well, that's exactly what happened and so we won the Battle of Anzio. Records of women in labour were playing all along the beaches.'

I had adapted *I Claudius* and *Claudius the God* – two books to which I had long been devoted – for the stage, and the play was directed by Tony Richardson, in whose house I met Robert Graves. To ensure the play's success he had brought a fragment of meteorite which he held in his hand.

'How will you get it to bring us good notices and a long run?' I asked him.

'I shall simply say to it, "Magic stone, do your job!"'

Perhaps it was the wrong formula, for the stone went off-duty on the first night and the play was a flop. But I shall always remember, with joy, discussing the well-known facts of history on a sofa with Robert Graves.

John Mortimer

Iris Murdoch

IN 1956 THE RANK Organisation asked me to direct my first film, and I was busy looking for a subject and reading new books. Iris Murdoch's first novel, *Under the Net*, had just been published. It was a combination of wild, original comedy and philosophical dissertation.

I had a friend in the story department of the studio called Kenneth Cavander and told him of my enthusiasm for the book, even though the philosophy was above most people's heads. Kenneth had just come down from Oxford, where he had been a Balliol scholar, and shared my enthusiasm. More importantly, he knew Iris Murdoch well enough to introduce me to her.

To my delight, she responded, saying it would be most interesting to discuss the possibility of a film of her first novel, so Kenneth arranged for us to meet in Oxford on Saturday.

She said she would meet us at the Randolph Hotel for lunch. We arrived early and sat in the restaurant waiting for her. A few minutes after one o'clock she hadn't arrived, so Kenneth went off to telephone her house.

He returned a few minutes later and said she sent her apologies for being late but unfortunately she had run over her husband with the car in the garage. She would be along shortly, and we were no to worry that she was letting us down. Her husband, John Bayley, the literary don, had been in the garage when Iris went to start up the car and drive out. Unfortunately he had been standing in front of the car: Iris put it in forward gear, not reverse, and pinned John to the wall.

She reassured Kenneth that there was absolutely no reason for us to cancel our lunch, nor delay it for more than ten minutes or so. Kenneth had tried to get more details about what had happened but she was quite unfussed and passed the incident off as unimportant.

When she arrived at the hotel she was perfectly calm and surprised at our interest in the accident, refusing to discuss the matter further beyond reassuring us that John would be quite all right.

She and Kenneth chattered away through lunch, mostly about Oxford gossip. Then we got to talking about the possibility of a film. I told her that I thought the story, the characters and the comedy could make a very funny, fresh and original film, but that the philosophical discourse would be too specialised for cinema audiences. She attempted a simplification, but I explained that for a film we needed less dialogue and more visual scenes. Yes, she understood that very well, there was clearly too much talk, and too much philosophy might not be popular, but the philosophy was important to her and couldn't just be cut. We parted the best of friends, and she promised to do her best to help with the problem.

I received a postcard saying that she had been able to solve both problems in one. She would keep the philosophy but change the subject to Buddhism, then we could have Buddhist mottoes all round the walls of the sets. That would do away with lots of talking, and, what's more, be very nice and visual.

It was an ingenious manipulation of possibilities which had its practical side, but like her choice of gears it did not lead us in a desirable direction and, alas, I never made the film.

Clive Donner

Salvador Dalí

IT WAS JUNE 1976. My wife and I were staying in Rosas on Spain's Costa Brava. Driving along a coast road we passed a black Cadillac with black windows. Was it the local Mafia, I joked to our English friend, who lived locally. No, it was the Dalís' chauffeur-driven car – 'He lives a few miles from here, in Port Lligat.'

Next morning, of course, we set off for the fishing village of Port Lligat. The Dalís' villa, screened by a high wall, was dominated by four enormous shapes on the rooftop – two white eggs and two metallic-grey human heads, both bald. Near the front entrance was a rotting rowing-boat, home to an emaciated mother cat and four kittens.

A Spanish photographer seemed to be waiting for something to happen. Three *Guardia Civil*, shouldering carbines, regarded us suspiciously. Moored at a jetty was a bright yellow motor-launch called *Gala*. Two men were getting it ready. I primed my camera.

Suddenly two bodyguard types came out of the house. Then the great Surrealist himself emerged, wearing a wide-brimmed straw sunhat, pale blue bathrobe and sandals. Close behind came his Russian-born wife, Gala, in white blouse and tight-fitting shorts, her black hair pinned up with a Tillie bow.

Pale and frail-looking at 72, Dalí spotted our cameras. 'Pictures of Dalí, yes,' he announced, 'but no pictures of *la señora.*' Gala smiled coyly and covered her face with a towel. The Dalís, in a rare public appearance, were off to a secluded cove for a swim.

As I snapped him he fixed me with the famous bulbous-eyed stare. Where was I from? London, I said. 'You come from London to see Dalí?' Indeed I had, I fibbed. He gave his famous moustache a twirl. 'I am not very beautiful now. Come back at eight tonight. I will make myself and my moustache beautiful for you.' He had what looked like a yellow fish-bone in his hand.

At 8pm we were met at the door by Enrique Sabater, who introduced himself as Dalí's personal assistant. 'Señor Dalí is waiting for you.' Then, to my wife, 'but not you.'

'Why not?' I demanded. Sr Sabater shrugged. 'Señora Dalí...she not like other ladies.'

I followed Sabater through a labyrinth of patios, ornamental gardens, narrow white-washed corridors with black and white stone steps. 'No interview,' Sabater said over his shoulder, 'and two pictures only.' The Dalís and a young man and a young woman were lolling on cushions under a canopy beside a phallic-shaped swimming pool. Gala had changed into a red blouse and black slacks; Dalí, his moustache waxed, wore a white frilly shirt and brocade waistcoat. Nobody stood up. Dalí introduced the young people as 'my favourite models, David and Suzanne'.

Dalí was holding up the 'fish-bone'. It was, he said, his latest creation – a wax model of a young man on a dolphin. He had done it on the boat that day; he would have it copied in gold and have precious stones embedded in it.

Could I take a group picture? Yes, but not of *la señora*! Would the maestro be coming to London in the near future? Sr Sabater snapped: 'No questions – just two pictures!' After I'd taken my snaps, Dalí said: 'Now you take a glass of wine with us.' A flunkey brought pink champagne and glasses. Three or four swallows and my audience was over.

Outside, I found my wife feeding a tin of sardines to the cats in the boat. 'You'd think,' she said, 'that with all his money he could give these poor mites a home.' Not so loud, I said. She'd get us both arrested.

Our Dalí adventure was not quite over. Next day, with our English friend we were invited to tea at Dalí's sister Ana Maria's house in near-by Cadaqués. She did not approve of Gala's or Sabater's influence on her brother: 'She has cast a spell on him; and he, Sabater, dominates him.'

As we left, Ana Maria signed a post-card print of a painting her brother had done of her: 'In the days,' as she put it, 'before Gala bewitched him.' It's a treasured souvenir.

Tony Wilmot

James Goldsmith

IN 1959 I WAS a student in need of a lucrative summer job. For reasons that are now unclear, I believed that the *Times* personal column was the best source of well-paid employment.

My intuition proved correct when I spotted an advertisement for 'Attractive young ladies, outdoor types, needed for exciting project, duration three months. Excellent remuneration.' I applied, emphasising my love of the outdoors and enthusiasm for riding, and shortly afterwards was invited to an interview by the sales manager of Ellanby Laboratories.

He commented that I was rather pale for one so much in the open air, but supposed it had been a damp spring. He then told me that my employer would be Jimmy Goldsmith, 'of whom you may have heard'. Indeed I had. A year or so earlier, Goldsmith, well-known as an extremely rich playboy and gambler, had eloped with the 17-year-old daughter of a Bolivian tycoon. Following a hasty marriage, she had tragically died in childbirth, leaving a baby daughter. Now it seemed that the bereaved husband had put his flamboyant past behind him. He was to devote himself to his daughter and start a business career. As a first step he had bought a respected but unprofitable chain of chemists called Lewis & Burroughs. They were also manufacturing chemists, and it was this aspect of the business that Mr Goldsmith was anxious to expand. Hence Ellanby Laboratories, and the exciting new product that I, and five other attractive, healthy outdoor types, had been hired to promote.

Jimmy Goldsmith himself presided over the first meeting of his new sales force. He asked about our recent holidays – it appeared that I was the only one of the group who had not recently returned from the Mediterranean. I remember the eligible widower as thin and rather pale – not an outdoor type himself.

Our product, he said, looking carefully at our complexions, was something quite new, a lotion to make you tan without the sun. It was called Night Tan, and you applied it before you went to bed at night, waking up to find yourself with a deep copper tan. He then went over the economics of Night Tan. It was to retail at 25 shillings, a very large sum in 1959. However, the more expensive a beauty product, the better it sold. Purchase tax accounted for five shillings of the cost, as did the retailer's margin. Production and marketing (us) were 2/3d and the actual ingredients cost 3d. A whacking 12/6d, said Jimmy proudly, was profit. There were no competitors.

The sales strategy was simple. Ellanby Laboratories had mailed six bottles of Night Tan to every retail chemist in the country, along with an invoice for £6. If they sold them all, they would make 30 shillings, and hopefully order more. If they did not sell, they could be returned.

Returns were to be strongly discouraged, and this was where we came in. Attractively tanned, we were to call on all the chemists, exulting in the effectiveness of Night Tan. In 1959, most people spent their holidays in damp Britain and sun lamps were unheard of. Only a few sales were needed for the secret to be out, and Night Tan would fly from the shops. Or so the theory went.

Unfortunately, there was just one flaw, which explained Goldsmith's insistence on horsey outdoor types. Night Tan did not turn you a deep copper bronze. It made you bright yellow, as if you had jaundice. I discovered this before the rest of the sales force. Being paler than the others, I went straight home and covered myself in the stuff. My first calls on the chemists were very unsuccessful. When Jimmy Goldsmith saw me, he was quite cross. I obviously needed to relax and ride more in my spare time – without a cap on.

The summer progressed. I visited every chemist in Kent and Sussex. As my natural tan deepened I made a few sales and some commission, but it was hardly 'excellent remuneration'.

By the end of the summer there were at least six other tan-without-the-sun products in the shops, all of them much cheaper than Night Tan. Nevertheless, Jimmy Goldsmith was pleased with the success of his business venture. He quietly killed off Night Tan and went on to buy Cavendish Foods and Marmite.

Kim Clark

Tom Stoppard

IN THE MID 1960s, when being tired and emotional meant your name was George Brown, I shared a mansion flat with friends on the wrong side of Vincent Square. Gently perfumed with boiled cabbage and old feet, the building sheltered a motley lot of dipsomaniacs, bisexuals, ex-Tory ministers, and trench coats from the MI6 office round the corner on Vauxhaull Bridge Road. Going to and from work we would furtively eye each other in the corridors, and at weekends would even risk a nod when lifting in the milk that was still, in those far-off days, delivered by a cheery milkman who doffed his cap and said 'Good morning, sir.'

One of the denizens of this Edwardian sepulchre was a lean young man, barely older than myself, who scurried in and out at odd hours dressed in a black velvet jacket and trousers that aged noticeably over the months. Pale and intense, with raven hair that curled wildly around his pallid features, he was obviously drawn by some unseen force that propelled him along the corridors like the March Hare. Sometimes he would be seen with a small child, or a woman, or both. The three lived directly above us, and often we would hear the child crying. Rumour had it that he was artistic.

At this time, as a novitiate in the Foreign Office, I kept gentleman's hours, which meant that crises never happened before ten o'clock and a full reading of the *Times*. So everyone else had left for work when there was a knock at the door and I opened it to find the black velvet suit. Its occupant smiled, apologised for the intrusion, and asked if we might do him a favour. He had, he explained, noted that we were out during the daytime. As a writer whose concentration was distracted by a crying infant, could he possibly use our kitchen table to write on during the day, when everyone was out? I should explain that the table was a bit of a sore point. For some mystical reason, one of my flatmates, an expert on medieval theology, had ordered one that was eight feet square. The result was no floor space and a table that could seat the twelve disciples. It definitely needed more using. So to get rid of the eccentric scribbler, I said yes. I didn't even bother with his name.

For the next few months I saw nothing of him. The only reminder of his existence was the coffee cup he always left unwashed in the sink and the unending litter of crumpled paper he threw into the wastepaper basket. Once I inspected it, only to find that every sheet was blank. This confirmed me in my pin-striped view that he was a wastrel, and I went about my own business of saving the world with an increased sense of purpose.

Then, one evening, he called to say he had completed his manuscript. 'Manuscript?' I echoed, not quite believing my ears and thinking of the forests he'd massacred in our kitchen. 'Oh, yes,' he smiled, 'I've been writing a play.' He must have seen the disbelief on my face. 'It's about a couple of characters from Shakespeare,' he explained, 'what happens behind the scenes.' Deranged, I thought, but felt compelled to be polite. 'Oh, who?' I asked. 'Rosencrantz and Guildenstern,' he replied, 'from *Hamlet*.' I looked at the decayed velvet suit and big black eyes staring at me from his mop of hair. Then I knew he was crazy.

David Stafford

Louis Armstrong

HE FIRST APPEARED here at the Holborn Empire, some time around 1945, as I remember. Then he was known as a 'jazz' player, so this hand-kerchief-waving, perspiring, coloured star was a little too *outré* for the Palladium. He was featured down the road at Moss Empire's No 2, as a soloist fronting a group of hand-picked British swingers.

Their string-bass player was Spike Hughes, also an A&R man, who led one of our first jazz groups recording on a major label, his 'Deccadents'. At the time I was pestering him to give me lessons and actually had a few, mostly with a cue on the snooker tables in the Six Bells, next to the record-ing studio. On this occasion, Spike asked me to help him.

He had a morning session to record the Ambrose band with Evelyn Dahl singing, and he feared possible difficulties and even rewriting of the musical arrangements to get them together. So he asked me to go to the theatre in case he was delayed, get his fiddle ready and stand by to deputise. Of course he made it, so we stood outside Louis' dressing-room listening to the wonderful, unforgettable sound of him warming up, together with his band.

When that smiling, jovial face full of flashing teeth came out and joined us, Satchmo was carrying a cigarette twice as fat and as long as any Craven A, and he passed it round for us whiteys to try. He had been brought up on the stuff – one of his finest recordings was entitled 'Muggles', another name for pot.

But when one of his now happy backing group went for a second drag, that smiling face turned livid. Almost viciously he grabbed back the roach, shook it in the offender's face and spat out: 'Man, if you use dat shit, you use dat shit, you don't let dat shit use you!'

Bob Lord

The Duke of Windsor

THE DUKE, as usual by teatime, was drunk. Not very drunk, but sufficiently soft in the head to have driven his Cadillac convertible along the fairways of Nassau's premier golf club. This was before electric buggies. Evidently he was not in the mood for long walks between shots; and, after all, he was the Governor. He was still HRH the Duke of Windsor, and I was an 18-year-old Pilot Officer, still easily impressed. He had given me a friendly wave as he drove his car past me on the 16th fairway.

He finished his game quickly and was well ahead of me in the bar. In the early stages of drinking, he had a charmingly whimsical, some said boyish, slightly tilted smile. Free for the afternoon from the Duchess's surveillance, he was able to indulge in playful informality. 'Hope you didn't mind my playing through,' he said. 'What'll you have?'

It was gratifying to be recognised by someone so senior, and astonishing to be offered a drink. We were both in civilian clothes, but they did not disguise the disparity of ranks – I in a white shirt and khaki trousers, he in a lime-green shirt and doeskin slacks of Schiaparelli shocking pink. After more than one drink, he became quite chatty, asking some of the questions that strangers ask in casual bar-room encounters: what's your name? where are you from? what do you do? 'A navigator, eh?' he commented. 'That must be jolly interesting. Astronomy and mathematics and so on. Training on Mitchells?' 'No, sir. Ferrying.'

'Ah! Trips to Egypt and India. I envy you.'

Since Churchill had ordered the Duke to assume the governorship, he was confined to the Bahamas. The Prime Minister was determined to prevent the ex-King from attempting to negotiate peace with Germany to help his friends there to fight more effectively against Communism.

'Come on,' he now said to me. 'Let's go for a ride.' Coming from him, the suggestion seemed very much like an order. 'You've been Over the Hill, I suppose.' 'Not yet,' I admitted, as suavely as possible. Over the Hill was a district, I had heard, that airmen and others sometimes daringly visited after dark. It was the black ghetto, noted for furtive all-night revelry in she-beens and shanties. Over the Hill was where the colony hid poverty, where the haves, for fun, went slumming with the have-nots. In this respect, the ghetto was like Harlem in the distant past.

I knew that the Duke of Windsor had the reputation of a fun-lover, a bit of a sport. He enhanced this reputation by encouraging Blind Blake, Nassau's foremost calypso singer, to perform as a sort of court jester at parties, even in Government House, accompanying himself on guitar and singing his popular new song, 'Love Alone':

Love, love alone,
Caused King Edward to leave the throne.
I know King Edward was noble and great,
But his love caused him to abdicate.
He got the money and he got the talk
And the fancy walk that would suit New York...

The Duke always led the laughter and applause.

But now I looked at my watch. Wasn't 4.45 rather early for this expedition? Part-way down the far side of the hill, I was surprised when the Duke produced an army cap with the scarlet band of superior rank and jammed it jauntily on his well-groomed fair head. He turned off the main road, along a narrow, unpaved road with a row of dilapidated wooden shacks on each side, and announced his arrival with long blasts on the horn – baaaahp! baaaahp! baaaahp!

I must have looked alarmed. 'It's all right,' he assured me. 'They know me. I come here often.' Several front doors opened promptly, as if his signal had been expected. Small boys, one by one and in twos and threes, ran out and gathered in the road near the car. There were about 15 of them, ranging in age from, say, eight to 12. They were dressed in cotton shirts and shorts that looked faded by many launderings, and they were all carrying rifles – that is to say, home-made facsimiles and sticks that represented rifles.

The Duke stood up in the car, a short, upright, slim figure of paradoxical dignity, the authoritative cap transcending the gaudy green shirt and pink slacks. The expression on his face was stern. Without any preliminaries, he commanded the boys, in a high-pitched yet military shout, to 'Fall in!' They duly obeyed, forming fairly straight ranks.

Then the Duke proceeded to drill them in accordance with the protocol of the Brigade of Guards. When he ordered them to 'Slo-ope ... arms!' they propped their toy rifles on their tiny shoulders very nearly in unison. When he yelled, 'By the left, qui-ick ... march!' they quickly marched, and the order 'A-bout ... turn!' soon got them back again.

When at last he stood them at ease and then easy, the boys were more like boys as they scrambled for the silver coins that their commander scattered in front of them.

How His Excellency laughed! I thought then that he was an awful fool, but I was grateful to him, and I am still, for demonstrating so vividly that warfare, or at least his part in it, was absurd.

Patrick Skene Catling

Stanley Baldwin

WHEN I WAS at Shrewsbury School before and during the war, the Headmaster liked to be known as Major H H Hardy. But this rigidly erect figure, with his long, narrow face, hands and feet, his hypnotically dominating eyes, as of some feral animal, behind pince-nez worn on a black ribbon, and his sinewy body invariably encased in a dark suit, all three of its buttons done up, was the very model not so much of a modern Major as of a modern Major-General. Even his custom of riding round the grounds at a sedate pace on a high, old-fashioned bicycle in no way detracted from his martial dignity. On a notable occasion he addressed the whole school on the subject of a boy who had been summarily 'sacked'. None of us was sure precisely what the boy had done. But when Hardy fulminated: 'I will not have hobbledehoys skulking together in secret in dark corners,' we at once knew.

Yet, like the school itself, Hardy was not all that he seemed. Both headmaster and school presented an authoritarian image, intolerant of anything that might be regarded as unpatriotic, namby-pamby, arty or, as in the case of the expelled boy, 'immoral'. Yet, in each case, behind that image something far more liberal lurked. Although I was one of those boys – a swot, a muff, a pacifist – for whom one would have imagined that Hardy would have had no use at all, there slowly emerged an odd rapport between us.

During my second year I won the annual French Prize. Hardy was standing at Stanley Baldwin's elbow when I mounted the platform to receive my prize at the annual Speech Day. That someone as distinguished as Baldwin was there at all was a tribute to Hardy's remarkable skill as a fixer. Baldwin had recently ceased to be Prime Minister, but he was still revered and loved by the country at large because, with all the slippery adroitness of a Wilson or Macmillan, he had weathered the General Strike, secured complete adult suffrage and carried public opinion with him over the Abdication. The years of humiliation, when his enemy Beaverbrook was, with malevolent glee, to order the demolition of the iron gates to the Baldwin estate on the pretext that they were needed for wartime scrap, were still ahead.

With his tufty eyebrows, similar to Denis Healey's, he looked like a well-fed badger. His face was far more mobile than I had expected from its suety appearance in newspaper photographs and newsreels. His fingernails were far from clean. Behind him, stiff-backed on a chair, was his dumpy wife, in the kind of elaborate garden-party hat, high in the crown and broad of brim, that could be seen on the head of almost every mother, including mine, in the Alington Hall on that summer's afternoon.

I cannot now remember what Baldwin said in the speech that preceded the prize-giving. But he spoke largely about the beauties of the countryside, and inevitably mentioned the three most distinguished Shrewsbury alumni – Sir Philip Sidney, Charles Darwin and Samuel Butler. His voice, though veiled by the huskiness of advancing years and unassisted by a microphone, was clear and strong.

The prizes were not in cash but in books – selected beforehand by the recipients up to the value of each prize. One of my choices was Housman's *Last Poems*. Baldwin had said merely a few words to each previous recipient, but the sight of the Housman on top of the small pile of books that he was about to hand over to me clearly interested him. He turned over some of the pages, even seemed to be reading for a moment. Then he asked me if I liked Housman's work. I was an enthusiast then as I am now and, blushing and stammering, I said that yes, yes, I liked him very much, he was one of my favourite poets. He then asked me which of his poems I liked best.

I told him that it was the one that begins 'With rue my heart is laden...'. His comment was: 'How strange that someone as young as you should pick on that!' We continued to talk for a while, until, no doubt aware that both Hardy and the audience were getting impatient, he handed over the pile of books and I returned to my seat.

After the ceremony, when I was standing with my mother and sisters on the lawn outside the Hall, one of the school prefects hurried over to tell me: 'Hardy wants to see you.' Hardy and the Baldwins were surrounded by some of the governors and staff at the far end of the lawn. My first thought was that I had done something wrong. But the reason for my summons turned out to be that among my other books Baldwin had noticed a copy of Mary Webb's *Seven for a Secret*. Unlike Housman, Webb is not an author whom I or many other people now admire; but at that time, largely due to Baldwin's championing of her work in a preface that he wrote for her *Precious Bane*, she was hugely popular. I was far too nervous for the ensuing conversation about her and her Shropshire to be a success. It proceeded jerkily and inconsequentially, until Baldwin made it clear that it was time for it to end. I then hurried off.

What now strikes me is the change between the circumstances of that far-off era and those of today. It may well be that a present-day former Prime Minister would be familiar with the works of, say, Ted Hughes and Beryl Bainbridge. But if he were so, instead of discussing them with a 15-year-old, he would probably decide that some subject less esoteric – say, pop music or football – would go far down better. Only two major politicians of recent times, Roy Jenkins and Denis Healey, have made absolutely no attempt to conceal their wide general culture; and my guess is that that is why neither has ever led the Labour Party.

Am I the only person who nowadays sighs for the uncommon touch among our politicians?

Francis King

Richard Widmark

HE WAS STANDING in front of me in the queue, waiting to rent a car from Avis. Short, very short, tanned and lined, he wore a narrow-brimmed hat with a hint of Florida golf courses about it, the kind of thing Bing Crosby used to favour, and the standard issue light-coloured raincoat, American tourists for the use of...

Except that this was no tourist. The queue shuffled closer to the counter. He waited his turn patiently. The faded blue eyes took in the rental rates and details of the Ford Escort 1.3L. He seemed... interested. This can't be, I thought.

I knew this man though I'd never queued with him before. I'd watched him from cheesy stalls in countless fleapits through the '40s and the '50s; snake-laughed psychopath in *Kiss of Death*, leathery US Marine 'blasting the Nips' in *Halls of Montezuma*, proficient and credible gunslinger in countless Westerns, gritty cop in Don Siegel's *Madigan*. And here he stood, waiting for an Avis Escort.

His wait was nearly over. The Avis doll – were they hand-picked for this Mayfair flagship? – pressed her inner switch and the Avis smile came on, just like in training, trying hard to show she was trying harder.

I couldn't catch the way it started. Heard all she said but nothing of him, apart from a murmur and mutter. At one point his hand went to his pocket, but he didn't floor her with a single blap from a .45 Colt automatic. He just fished out a biro.

So she shuffled her forms and said brightly, in a trying-harder kind of way, 'Name?' And he said, 'Widmark.' And she said, without a glimmer of reaction, 'W-I-D... ?' And he spelled it out for her and she wrote it down and then said, 'Christian name?' And he said, 'Richard,' and she repeated 'Richard,' and wrote that down on the form too, her tongue in the corner of her mouth.

And no-one else in that branch of Avis in North Row knew, showed any sign of knowing, that this small and patient man, biro in hand, was Widmark the movie actor, sniggering killer, occasional hero, cowboy, cop. Big screen, big name, famed, a legend...

Except me – I knew. And then as the blonde curls bounced over the Avis forms, the washed blue gaze checked out the scene as though for hoods and trouble. Behind him the Avis doll said, 'Your vehicle will be with you momentarily, Mr uh... '

'Widmark,' he said again, and with that grinned at me because he knew I knew. Grinned that cheek-drawn, toothy, vulpine grin that took me back to the fag-fogged shillings in the Ritz. The grin he grinned from under snap-brimmed fedoras, GI helmets, Stetsons black and white...

Then he moved outside, by the garage doors where the cars arrived, and climbed aboard his shiny, trying-harder bright red Escort and motored mildly away.

Later I worked out what film he'd been making on that trip, and it was rotten. He was good though, tough, convincing, Richard Widmark movie ikon, not Mr uh Widmark in the queue. But older, worn and older and it showed.

Now when I see him on the box it summons up for me glimmers of '82, waiting in the Avis queue. Most recently I saw a Western, *Last Wagon* from 1957. 'You lived in it... you fought in it... you loved in it... and sometimes you died in it,' cried the blurb on first release. In real life, as only I can testify, the wagon was an Escort 1.3L.

Frank Barnard

Bertrand Russell

IN SEPTEMBER 1948, as a reporter on what we were proud to call the *Manchester Guardian*, I was on holiday in Trondheim, Norway, with a local journalist, Eystein Dohl. Such was the prestige of the *Guardian* that Eystein interviewed me for his paper (he was paid on lineage!), and as a result the students' union at the university invited me to a lecture by Bertrand Russell.

For two days we had endured high winds and driving rain. On the morning of Russell's arrival we were surprised by the number of ambulances racing through the town. Someone told us that in the wind a seaplane had crashed into the fjord drowning 19 people. Also, a famous British philosopher was on board. After that, Eystein and I moved faster than the wind. Russell had been taken to an hotel where the manager would not let us see him. Fortunately the president of the students' union was about to visit him and he took us in with him.

We learned that Russell had sat at the rear of the plane so that he could smoke his pipe. Those in front could not escape when the plane nose-dived into the water but someone pushed Russell through a window and he swam around in the icy fjord for two or three minutes before being picked up.

So there he was sitting up in bed, reading a thriller and smoking a pipe. He looked extraordinarily elfish and apologised for being in bed, due, he said, to having been up at an 'unchristian' hour to catch the plane.

His nonchalance was amazing for a man of 76 after such a terrifying experience, but it seemed to me that he was enjoying the limelight and the admiration of everyone around him.

'I always wondered what I would say in such a situation,' he said. 'I imagined I would say something extreme like "damnation!" but, you know, all I said was "well, well". Nobody asked me if I could swim. They just pushed me unceremoniously out of a window.'

Quaking at the effrontery of such a question, I asked, 'Can you swim?'

'Of course I can,' he replied indignantly. 'But it is a little difficult in one's overcoat. Also I was trying to hang on to my attaché case but in the end I had to let it go. Now I have no papers but so far no-one seems to doubt that I am me.'

Nor did they. Later he gave his lecture on 'Ideologies and Common Sense.' Whatever his merits as a philosopher, the students thought he was a great and brave man.

As for me my main anxiety was how to get the story to Manchester out of my £35 allowance. There were severe limits on money for foreign travel in those days but my Norwegian friends rallied round and my reward came later when I bought a *Manchester Guardian* in Stockholm and saw my scoop displayed prominently on the front page.

Stephen Parkinson

Hugh MacDiarmid

THE SPECULATIVE society, whose anteroom, debating hall and library are just inside the entrance to Old Court, within, but not part of, Edinburgh University, was founded in 1764 'for the improvement of literary composition and public speaking.' Its members have included Sir Walter Scott and RL Stevenson, Lord Brougham and Lord John Russell, Prince Alfred, Duke of Edinburgh and Prince William of Hesse (both great-uncles of Prince Philip), many luminaries of the Scottish legal profession, some of the medical profession, and a few 'industrials' – like me.

In the later '40s, when I was elected, few Speculators had a taste for Hugh MacDiarmid's writings, and fewer if any were in sympathy with his political views. Times change; by 1964 when the Society celebrated its bicentenary with a grand banquet he had become a celebrity, a national figure, and had been elected the Society's Honorary Bard.

At the banquet he was invited, because of a known tendency to become less coherent during the course of an evening, to declaim after the first course from a central position at high table. His brilliant contribution, partly in verse, partly in prose, was loudly applauded as he resumed his place on the outermost sprig at which I sat a few places away.

Dinner proceeded, after which the Duke of Edinburgh, an Honorary Member, rose to speak. Scarcely had he begun than H MacD started to interject: 'Nonsense!... What's he saying?... Never heard such rubbish' etc etc. Prince Philip weathered all this with good humour. Shortly afterwards the Honorary Bard lapsed into silence, then fell off his chair and lay prostrate.

I and another member, who was medically qualified, rushed to assist him. The doctor, having quickly ascertained that there was no cause for particular alarm, took the legs, I took the shoulders and we carried the little body through an adjacent side exit. Just outside this, a large empty laundry hamper was ready to receive the evening's napery, so we popped him in to sleep it off, returned to our places and listened to the rest of the proceedings, which had continued uninterrupted.

The Honorary Bard suffered no ill effects and lived to write, rant and drink until his eighty-sixth year.

Michael Strachan

George Orwell

IT MUST HAVE been around the early 1930s that the gentleman char came into my mother's life. I helped her in the house after school, as had my older sisters, but they were now out at work. How she coped, in that old, cold, inconvenient, no-amenities house was truly amazing. We were a family of ten, with huge appetites, and we frequently brought hungry friends home for meals. My mother could stretch a meal quite miraculously. We lived in Limehouse, close to the docks (the area now featured in the TV soap *EastEnders*).

One day a friend who lived near Whitechapel's Rowton House, a hostel for the homeless, brought 'Laurel' to our house. His real name was not known; 'Laurel' was the label attached to him by the East Enders with whom he came into contact. He was prepared to clean our house for the going rate of half a crown (12½ pence) a day, plus a midday meal. The money just about covered the cost of a bed at Rowton House, and possibly some cigarettes.

I came home early one afternoon and there he was. The tall, slim, narrow-faced 'charman' bore a resemblance to the Laurel of the much-loved comedy partnership Laurel and Hardy.

The man spoke to me. It was not what he said that startled me, it was the way he said it. His speech was what we at that time called Oxford English, cultured, correct, plum-in-the-mouth BBC English. I was too young then to hide my surprise at his posh accent. He smiled gently, bowed slightly, and then further astonished me by kissing my mother's hand and saying, 'Goodbye, queen of the kitchen.' Turning to me he added, 'Your mother is a fine lady and a splendid cook.'

My mother was consumed with pity for the poor man. She told me that he had scrubbed all the floors, cleaned the twin outside lavatories and polished the blacklead cooker to a mirror finish. 'That well-bred gentleman worked so hard I had to make him stop for a rest.'

Then, quite suddenly, Laurel vanished. He was seen no more in our part of the East End. He was just another of the anonymous men who overnighted at the doss house.

After the last war, I came upon a book written by George Orwell. In it was a photograph of the author, taken when younger. The man was Eric Blair, and I recognised him. He was my mother's Laurel; it must have been during his period of tramping around London, doing any work that came his way, that he did his East End charring.

George Orwell was reputed to have said that the women he admired most were the hardworking, uncomplaining mothers of at least eight children. I like to think that he included my mother in this. She certainly fitted the description.

Stella Judt

Enid Blyton

I WAS TEN and the school holidays were becoming monotonous. I had re-read all my *Famous Five* books. Now, like George and the others, I wanted an adventure. So I decided to call on the author of the *Famous Five* – Enid Blyton.

The week before, I had been taken on a coach trip to Beaconsfield, where the prolific children's writer lived in Penn Road. After visiting the model village – the object of the trip – I had persuaded my aunt and uncle to stroll along Penn Road in search of Green Hedges, the author's home. And suddenly, there it was, exactly as pictured in Enid Blyton's own magazine that most of the pupils in my class read avidly. I stood at the gate and gaped, willing her to come out. She didn't.

A short time before this, a poem I'd submitted had won first prize and had been published in *Sunny Stories*. I'd called it 'Enid Blyton's Party' and incorporated in it the names of many of the characters from her books. On the strength of this, I reasoned that she would be pleased to see me. We could chat about my poem, and then about *The Adventurous Four, Bumpy and his Bus, Mr Galliano's Circus* and all the folk of *The Magic Faraway Tree*. Perhaps she'd give me a hint as to what the Famous Five would be up to next. That would be something to tell the kids at school. How envious they'd all be.

I set off on my Raleigh upright bicycle to follow the route that the Smith's Luxury Coach tour had taken the previous week. It was a long haul. But I was fortified by the reception I imagined I'd be given when I got to Beaconsfield.

'So you're the child who wrote that amusing poem – well done! And you've cycled all the way from Reading to see me? You must stay to tea!' Enid Blyton was bound to say, clapping her hands delightedly – adding, like a cosy character from her books, and with lots of exclamation marks, 'Ooooooooh! What tremendous fun we'll have! There will be four kinds of jam! Lemonade! Ice cream! And three different cakes!'

At last, hot, weary but triumphant, I reached her home in Penn Road. I carefully padlocked my bike to the slender trunk of one of the Green Hedges and, with a feeling of utmost excitement, walked up the drive to ring the bell.

But instead of Eeny Blyton, as she was affectionately known in my class, a maid opened the door. This threw me. I was suddenly tongue-tied.

'Er...excuse me, I...um...don't feel well.' I heard myself mumbling, in panic. 'Could I have a drink of water, please?'

Before the maid could respond, almost before I had taken in the large Chinese vase placed just ahead at the turn of the staircase, the writer herself appeared from a room on the left. The frizzy hair was unmistakable. She was wearing a New Look frock and had scarlet fingernails.

'What does this child want?' she asked, as if I were not there.

'He says he feels unwell, ma'am.'

Enid Blyton turned a concerned gaze towards me. 'Do you need a doctor? There's a doctor across the road.'

'No, no,' I stammered, 'I'll be all right if I drink some water. I just... feel sick!'

'Well, you mustn't be sick here!' she exclaimed firmly. 'Show him into the garden,' she told the maid.

I sprawled on the lawn, frustratedly staring at the back of the house. This wasn't the way I'd planned it. Out came the maid with a tumbler, a jug of water and a few boiled sweets on a tray. This was when, to my later shame, I recovered my composure and conversational skills.

'By the way,' I said chattily, as if suddenly discovering something. 'Wasn't that lady Eeny Blyton... the authoress?'

The maid gave me a shrewd look that turned into a smile. How many other star-struck children had pulled this one?

'Indeed it was,' she replied. 'She sent you these sweets to have with the water and said do stay – in the garden – and don't leave until you feel better. Goodbye!'

Not long afterwards I slunk away, unchained my bike and dawdled dejectedly down to Slough to catch the stopping train home.

I had met my literary idol, but where was the evidence? I had no autograph. No photograph signed 'To Terry, from Enid Blyton'. No 'Happy Snap' taken together. Only my word. And that wasn't enough for the kids at Grovelands School.

'Anyone could say that,' they scoffed, after the holidays, when I recounted my true-life Enid Blyton adventure. 'Bet you're only making it up.'

Terence Daum

H G Wells

THE HOUSE was no 13 Hanover Terrace, deliberately chosen to taunt the superstitious. The maid showed me to the 'sun-trap', a room at the top of the house which concentrated available sunshine. As I entered I could head Mozart playing and there, nodding asleep in front of the gramophone, was the man who had inspired my life – and millions of others – H G Wells. It seemed sacrilege to break into his sleep and so I waited until he became aware of my presence.

It was the gramophone which broke the impasse. It ground to a halt and the slurring of the needle brought him awake. He looked at me in some uncertainty and then said abruptly: 'Who the bloody hell are you?'

'I'm Brome – don't you remember we made a date for me to call?'

'But why interrupt me?' he said. ' Can't you see I am dying?'

He certainly was dying, with diabetes, a weak heart and but one whole lung and one kidney to live by. When his friends fell ill now, it became the occasion for a burst of bravado. As if these youngsters could hope to beat him at his own game – he who had been dying so long that nobody could hope to match the sustained achievements of sickness to which he had laid claim.

'Well,' he at last continued, 'what's it all about?'

'I'm writing a piece for the British Council about sustaining culture in wartime.'

'Culture! Oh my God! What does the word mean? Why not read this?' He pushed across to me a relatively slender manuscript. I glanced at the title, which I later checked: *Thesis on the Quality of Illusion in the Continuity of the Individual Life in the Higher Metazoa with Particular Reference to the Species Homo Sapiens.*

'Read it,' he said, ' and put it in your piece. If they had listened to me we wouldn't be in this mess now.' Only later did I realise that *they* in this context were the members of the Royal Society, who were still refusing to grant him an FRS. He said quite bluntly: 'That'll show the bastards!'

He was a wreck of his old self, a loosely knit accumulation of skin and bones, with his barrel of a forehead still dominating the face. But his reedy cockney voice continued to loose off broadsides in all directions.

He did so now: 'This farce of monarchy,' he said. 'You won't forget to put in your piece my detestation of monarchy, will you? Until we come to our senses about monarchy we won't get anywhere.'

In the middle of another more sustained diatribe he said, 'Let me show you the house.' It was a very remarkable house, reflecting so many sides of his personality.

We went first to the main bedroom. As befitted a man who had been a great lover and so careless about paternity, there was a four-poster bed with a canopy and curtain. On the mantelpiece stood photographs of the women who had been deeply part of his emotional life. Among the graceless concubinage of his mistresses, given pride of place, was the photo of Catherine, his second wife.

On the first floor we entered the famous ladies' room, lined with mirrors. In the lavatory, was a seat designed by himself at a special angle. In a separate room the private telephone exchange by which he could call Margaret the maid, Mrs Johnston the housekeeper, or anyone prepared to respond to his imperative summonses.

Down to the garage next, to have displayed with a touch of pride, artistic onslaughts by his own hand. They were crude sketches depicting the dawn of civilisation from beetle-like trilobites to man. Above them he had written: 'Have you the wits, have you the will to save yourselves?'

He continued his attacks as we moved from room to room. God was a superstitious irrelevance, parliament a democratic sham, Bernard Shaw a talented buffoon, women a necessary encumbrance to the life of man.

He knew that he was dying. 'Among the complications of my never very sound body is a fatty degeneration of the heart which ended the life of my father.'

The cheery, friendly soul people found in Wells's novels seemed to have little resemblance to this man. Until the very moment when he escorted me out of the front door he continued to issue judgements which sounded like last judgements on princes, prime ministers, and generals. As for humanity – it was 'a parcel of sweeps.'

'I never met such a chap,' said Shaw. 'I could not survive meeting such another.'

At the end of a two hour meeting I echoed his sentiments. How could this be the same man who wrote *The History of Mr Polly*, *Kipps*, *The War of the Worlds*, *The Time Machine* and *A Short History of the World*? How could this be the man who so powerfully contributed to the birth of the modern mentality? I never had another chance to answer those riddles.

Vincent Brome

EM Forster

ONE BRIGHT sunny day many years ago when I was living and teaching in Bishop's Stortford, a pretty young friend invited me to drive into Cambridge with her to do some essential shopping.

Her doctor husband was driving and, as parking was a problem, he put us down on the Backs and suggested that we should walk through the precincts of King's College into King's Parade.

My friend put her small son into the smallest of pushchairs and we passed through the massive gate. As we walked along the path we admired the beauty of the ancient lawn and the splendour of King's College Chapel in the sunlight. It was all so beautiful.

Suddenly the peace was destroyed by someone shouting 'Get back! Go away! How dare you!' I looked behind me to see if rowdy students were making a disturbance – and realised that we were the cause of this outburst of rage. A small, frantic old man in a long overcoat, cap and scarf was scuttling down the steps of an adjacent building, waving his stick in a threatening manner at us – two astonished young women and a startled baby.

'Can you not read?' he screeched. 'Do you not read notices? You are not allowed in these precincts with a perambulator!'

I could read. I had recognised this angry little figure at once as

Edward Morgan Forster. I had read all his books with great pleasure ('Only connect' his salient message).

I was not easily intimidated. Did I not deal with students every day of the week? My gentle friend was pink with embarrassment and totally silenced. I was not.

I said quietly: 'Do calm down or you will have a stroke.'

His mouth fell open in amazement and his entire manner changed. He said quite politely: 'You are not allowed in here with a wheeled vehicle. There is a notice on the gate. You must go back.' I replied: 'We are within a few yards of King's Parade and quite some distance from the gate through which we entered. Should we not wheel this small pushchair through the nearest exit?' 'Go on then,' he muttered, 'and don't do it again!'

I wish I had never met that most sensitive of writers, E M Forster.

Nonie Beerbohm

Sir Clifford Curzon

ONE SUMMER when I was about ten, my friend and I were looking for some amusement. The late Sir Clifford Curzon, pianist and chamber music player, lived next door to her house and each evening he would sit outside with a drink. We decided to ruin his peace and took to slipping into his huge garden and 'streaking' across his lawn at some distance from where he sat.

We imagined that he would rub his eyes in disbelief and look at his drink as if it were responsible for the sight of two naked girls dancing on the grass.

We continued tormenting him, and as my best friend's bedroom window looked over where he sat we decided to hang our repellent-looking teeth-braces out on bits of cotton and dangle them down like glistening clear plastic spiders. When Sir Clifford looked up with surprise and confusion we ducked behind the window, tears of laughter streaming down our faces.

My friend was absolutely mortified when her brace caught in the hedge and fell off. As it had cost a fortune, and she had already lost a good many, she decided that she would rather face the wrath of Sir Clifford than that of her mother.

We rang the door-bell and the butler answered. We explained what had happened, though not quite why we had been hanging our braces out of the window. We waited for a while and almost ran off. Half an hour later the butler returned with a red cushion, upon which sat a revolting plastic brace, two boiled sweets and a little note. The butler smiled and closed the door. We put the sweets in our mouths and walked back into her garden.

The note said: 'Leave me alone, keep your clothes on and no-one shall hear of this. PS: Never accept sweets from strange old men.' We decided from then on that it would be kinder to let him be old in peace.

Sophie Radice

Andy Warhol

IN THE early Eighties I was a chauffeur for a Mercedes car hire firm in West Berlin. One day I was sent to the Hotel Kempinski to pick up four customers and take them to East Berlin. When I arrived at the Kempinski I found that one of the four was Andy Warhol, who was in West Berlin to visit an exhibition in the Martin-Gropius-Bau. The others were a Canadian author whose name I have forgotten and two tattooed leather-and-steel clad gentlemen friends of the Canadian and Warhol. At first everything went OK. We drove through Checkpoint Charlie, made a compulsory money exchange, visited the usual tourist sights of East Berlin, the Pergamon Museum, Alexander Platz and, of course, the Russian cemetery in Treptow. On our way back to West Berlin I pointed out to Mr Warhol that none of us would be able to take our East German marks out of East Berlin. Warhol asked me what we could buy with the money and I suggested going to a souvenir shop. It was agreed and I drove them to a shop in Treptower Park. Warhol bought some kitsch, a replica of the TV tower at Alexander Platz. The Canadian also bought something small, but the two 'heavies' purchased quite an armful of presents between them – dolls, flags etc.

The trouble started when one of the boyfriends asked me to ask the shop assistant for another brown paper bag. (I should explain here that this was East Berlin, not Times Square, and that with his purchase each customer got one paper bag, and one only.) I explained the situation to lover-boy but he insisted that I should ask anyway. I did and, as I knew would happen, the request was refused. I translated this for angel-face and after looking heavenward for guidance he told me to ask that 'asshole' for a 'BROWN PAPER BAG – GODDAMIT' – which I did and was again refused. This went on for another couple of times, Warhol's friends getting progressively noisier. After a couple of 'Does she know who the fuck she is dealing with?' he slowly sank to his knees and with his hands held high, tears streaming down his face – he shouted at the top of his voice, 'All I want for Christ's sake is a fucking brown paper bag.'

A deathly silence fell over the shop. Warhol had a half grin on his face but I noticed one assistant saying to the other 'Call the *Stasi*' (secret police). I said to Warhol that if we didn't get away smartish we would all wind up in the huge complex at Alexander Platz that housed the *Staatssicher-heitsdienst* and that the least that would happen would be that we would have to cool our heels for a few hours for disturbing the peace. I reminded Warhol of his appointment that evening at the Martin-Gopius-Bau and told him we should leave immediately. The Canadian and the other fine example of American manhood dragged their by now hysterical friend back to the car, I raced to Checkpoint Charlie and we passed back into West Berlin and to the Kempinskki. On the way back, the Canadian started to sing that song that Bob Hope sang in the film *Pale Face* – 'East is East and West is West, and the wrong one I have chose.' Everybody started laughing (Warhol just grinned) and the hysterical one went back to being the lovely, broken-nosed, scarfaced, sweet young thing he was before. I was glad to see them get out of the car and out of my sight.

Robert Lowe

Oscar Hammerstein

IT WAS IN the early 1950s when the musicals of Rogers and Hammerstein were bringing a new vitality to the war-tired London stage. He had invited my wife and me to lunch with him at the Caprice restaurant, then London's most 'in' place for show-business folk. My own circumstances at the time were not nearly so glamorous. I too was rather war-tired and had recently undergone treatment for the dispersal of gastric ulcers. Thus I found myself seated in the cocktail bar at the Caprice gazing moodily at a glass of tonic water.

Hammerstein himself arrived before my wife, looking like a cross between a bare-fist fighter and an ageing all-America quarterback, his grey hair cut *en brosse* after the then-prevailing transatlantic fashion.

'Whassat you're drinking?' he demanded. I told him somewhat shamefacedly, and added that it was on medical advice.

'Sounds to me like the usual load of crap,' he said and, ordering himself a large something-or-other, proceeded to apply himself with flattering attention to my case history.

'Waal,' he said at last, with a touch of world-weariness, 'I sure cured Richard Rogers and I guess I'm gonna cure you.' A page boy was sent for. 'Go to the nearest chemist,' the great man instructed him, 'and buy the largest size of soluble capsule which they have in stock. On the way back stop and purchase a packet of Dreft washing powder.'

When the page returned with the required items, Oscar Hammerstein II filled one of the capsules with the then newly-marketed miracle washing powder and, handing it to me, commanded that I swallow it.

'Take one every morning for a while and you should be fine,' he prescribed with the air of a trusted family doctor. 'Now you can have some gin in that tonic water.'

I did as I was told and I must report that, although for some time afterwards bubbles came out of my ears whenever I blew my nose, I have never suffered from any more ulcer trouble, for going on 40 years.

Douglas Sutherland

Mrs Patrick Campbell

TO ME SHE looked an ordinary rather stout old woman. She was hard-up at the time and reduced to touring the provinces and suburbs with a small company acting the roles she had played when she was young and beautiful.

Her company was playing at the King's Theatre, Hammersmith. As we lived nearby, Mother, who though younger than her had been an admirer and longstanding friend, invited her to come to tea and have a rest between the matinée and evening performance, the final one of the season.

Her first words to me were, 'How old are you? What do you do?' I thought she was rather frightening and said timidly that I was nineteen and at art school, and she said, 'When I was your age I was supporting a husband and two children,' which made me feel very inadequate, and I left the room.

When it was time for her to leave, Mother called me and said, 'Mrs Pat wants you to go back to the theatre with her and act as her dresser.' (Her dresser had walked out on her after the matinée, a not unusual occurrence with her dressers, I heard later.) I was very alarmed as I had no idea how to 'dress' an elderly actress. However we went off to the theatre together in a taxi.

I managed to get her out of her dress, to reveal that underneath she was wearing a lace-up corset grey with age, and yellow celanese 'directoire' knickers, the elastic of which, having becoming slack with age, was tied in a knot at the waist. I managed to get her into her stage costume. There were lots of hooks and eyes in Victorian costumes! She was very preoccupied and taciturn, only speaking to me to bark out instructions. I didn't leave the dressing room when she was on stage and I don't remember what the play was, but it might have been *Magda*.

For the final act she wore a sequinned evening gown, the sight of which filled me with dismay as there were patches of plain material where sequins had fallen off and strands of black cotton with an odd sequin or two hanging on the end. I didn't know how she dared go on the stage in such a derelict garment. However, I managed to get her into it all right and she left the room.

Some time later I was told the curtain was about to come down, so I crept into the wings. I saw to my amazement a complete transformation had taken place. There in the spotlight stood an elegant and beautiful woman in a shimmering gown, the sequins sparkling in the lights. Bouquets of flowers surrounded her feet, one arm was filled with flowers, the other hand blowing kisses as she bowed and smiled at the audience, who were giving her a standing ovation with tumultuous clapping and cries of 'Bravo! Bravo!'

I was so impressed by this wonderful transformation that I remember it vividly to this day, although it took place nearly 70 years ago.

I never saw her again after that night.

Barbara Ker-Seymer

Donald Wolfit

IT WAS MORE than 50 years ago. The little old lady in tweed suit and felt hat who accompanied me to the matinée was my go-between. She had been a childhood friend of Don's from Newark days but how I came to know her and who precisely she was is a mystery. We went to see *Macbeth* or *Hamlet* or *Volpone*, I forget which, and had been graciously invited backstage.

We penetrated the dingy interior and mounted the stairs to the principal dressing-room. The door was not particularly memorable but the response to my friend's timid knock most certainly was: 'Enter!' He was seated on a very ordinary chair, surrounded by the costumes of his trade, but his relaxed pose and august presence filled the room. The chair became a throne. Our host ceased to be an actor and became a personification of the Prince Regent. I was not visiting, I was being presented.

After a polite exchange of greetings, he looked me up and down and said words to the effect: 'So this young man wants to go on to the stage. It is a great profession but unless you are called, you're wasting your time. And something must be done about that voice of yours,' – I had just returned to Oxford after four years' service as an officer – 'it reeks of privilege. What are you going to do when you carry a spear or pretend to be a ruffian? I can't imagine you saying: "Faith, sir, we were carousing till the second cock: and drink, sir, is a great provoker of three things." Say it.' I tried. 'No, no, that will never do. A mouse could do better.' I felt like one. 'Let me hear you breathe. Breathe! Enough. Here, put your hand here.' He pointed to a spot frighteningly close to his belly.

I was intimidated, so intimidated that I did as I was told. He inhaled a massive amount of air and the flesh concealed beneath his dressing-gown expanded to an alarming extent. I thought he was about to rise from the chair like a hot-air balloon, but slowly it began to subside as a low, melodic note issued from his mouth. It seemed to last an eternity.

Shortly after the demonstration, we were dismissed, not summarily but kindly. He had enjoyed impressing a young and naive aspirant to the profession. But it is his presence that I remember most vividly. Imagine someone who can dominate a great Victorian theatre with a whisper, who can demand applause by hanging onto the curtain like a silent opera singer, and then stuff such a man into a small dressing-room; be not surprised then that, as I descended the stairs, these words came to me: 'I could be bound in a nutshell, and count myself a king of infinite space...' Perhaps we had been to *Hamlet*, not to *Macbeth*. Who knows?

Robin Rook

Dr Hastings Banda

IN THE EARLY 1950s I was a medical student at a north London teaching hospital, a rather bleak Victorian brick building of some architectural importance. London teaching hospitals are not what they were – thank heavens. In those days they were medical power-houses. Patients came from all over the country, and the people attending them, students, nurses, and patients most especially, were made to feel that they were privileged to be there. Consultant staff were treated like gods, and some of them behaved as though this was only right and proper. As a result, patients were so tongue-tied they could hardly answer questions about their conditions.

Out patient clinics were run as follows. In a small echoing consulting room, wooden floored and walled with green and white tiles, would be a small wooden table with two chairs on one side – one for the Great Man and one for a student, who was there to take notes – and on the other a single chair for the patient (no relatives allowed). Behind were several tiered benches for students. Patients were led in by the clinic nurse, questions put by the consultant and findings noted by the student clerk. After this brief episode the patient would be led away to a small curtained cubicle to undress, lie under a blanket and wait for the consultant to come in and conduct an examination. Once his cubicles were full of undressed bodies under blankets, the consultant would examine each one, possibly allow a student or two to feel a lump, or listen to a heart murmur, and give his opinion to the patient. All this might take less than five minutes of actual consultation, though the patient could have been in the hospital for some hours.

One warm summer's afternoon, a clinic was being held, and I was the clerk for the day. Matters were proceeding normally and ten or so patients had been seen. The next patient was summoned.

A young African lady came into the room – an unusual occurrence in those days – strikingly attired in native dress. Her face was lined with three diagonal scars on each cheek, presumably tribal markings. She was very nervous. She complained of an outbreak of painful ulcers on her tongue and lips, which came on a week or so before her periods. Further questioning revealed that her periods had recently been painful and that she had taken some herbal tablets for the pain. The ulcers had appeared at that time.

A nice case with a ready solution which would have had a satisfactory outcome had matters been left there. But they were not.

The patient was led to a cubicle, there to undress, lie naked under a blanket and wait to be examined. When we arrived (consultant, nurse chaperone and about six male students) she was clearly terrified. Most of us were ashamed and embarrassed as a complete examination was undertaken; had the term 'gang rape' been in use at that time, it might have sprung to mind. The examination completed, she was told to stop the herbal remedy and we left. On returning to the consulting room, we had a short talk and sent for the next patient. The door opened, but instead of the expected patient, a short African man of about 50 appeared. He was immaculately dressed in black jacket and striped trousers – the morning suit that most of our consultants wore on their Harley Street days. He wore a Homburg hat, perhaps a size too large, and carried a tightly rolled umbrella with a brilliant yellow cane handle.

'You have disgraced and insulted my daughter by examining her with all these men present,' he said, waving his umbrella at us. 'You have behaved unethically.'

The consultant started to explain about the need for students to gain experience, but he did not get very far.

'You have disgraced her!' he thundered. Raising the umbrella above his head, he brought it crashing down on the table with such force that the handle broke off. The noise reverberated throughout the Department, after which there was a strange silence.

It had the effect of calming him and he picked up his umbrella together with the broken cane handle, walked to the door and opened it. Before leaving, he turned towards us and with some dignity said, 'I am Dr Hastings Banda. You will be hearing more of me.'

John Dudley Jenkins

Queen Mary

IN THE LATE SPRING or early summer of 1941, I was stationed in the area of Savernake Forest. I had been mended, restored and re-equipped following the Continental adventure of the previous year, and was awaiting posting to a new unit. I set out one afternoon to walk the two miles or so into Marlborough. As I ambled along, enjoying the afternoon, a large black car passed me and drew into the side of the road. A chauffeur alighted, walked back to me, saluted and said 'Her Majesty Queen Mary would like to give you a lift, Sir.'

Rather in a daze, I walked to the car and, indeed, there in the car was Queen Mary, unmistakable in her toque with her high-necked dress and a band around her neck. I climbed into the car and we moved off. There was a short silence and then she uttered, 'What is your name?' I told her. Another short silence. 'What is your regiment?' This information given she said, 'Good, good'. We drove on a little further. 'Do you write to your mother every week?' she demanded. 'I certainly try to, Ma'am.' 'Good, good,' she said.

We soon reached the centre of Marlborough. The car stopped, the chauffeur opened the door. I alighted, said, 'Thank you for the lift, Ma'am', and gave her my smartest salute. 'Good luck to you,' she said and drove off, leaving a rather bemused young soldier wondering who would believe him when he told the story in the mess. I discovered later that I was by no means the only one to be picked up by Queen Mary.

Leo Morris

Marlon Brando

YEARS AGO, a senior executive in the United Nations decided it would be a good idea to get the BBC interested in their celebration of the Year of the Child. He flew specially to London for discussions and, by a stroke of bad luck, I was invited to take it on. Fortunately I had just seen a copy of *Playboy* in which Marlon Brando had been expounding the importance of the care of children in the future of mankind. Perhaps he could front such a programme; he was on the UN's list of Hollywood's helpers. I wrote to Brando suggesting we meet to discuss the matter. A month or so later the telephone rang. It was Brando. Could I come and discuss things next Wednesday morning? After realising this was the real thing, and not some friend of the BBC playing tricks, I agreed.

Off I flew, wondering what I had let myself in for. On the Wednesday a taxi drove me to Mulholland Drive and stopped in front of barred gates, while the driver shouted into the entrance microphone. The gate swung open and the car was surrounded by several angry dogs. A smiling secretary called them off and I was ushered into a Japanese-style house to a chair in the open-plan sitting room. After a while a large figure in a bathrobe slowly strode in, put up a hand and sat down opposite me. I opened my mouth to speak – but again, up went the hand. What films had I made? I told him some titles and he picked up the telephone, rang the United

Nations in New York and asked for copies to be sent to him. I told him I could probably get them quicker through the BBC office, so the phone was passed to me and the process repeated. After some discussion he decided he wanted me to go round the world, visiting every country nonstop. I said, well, there was a programme budget to consider, even though he was not expecting a fee.

After a while he thought we might eat, so we retired to the small kitchen. On the refrigerator door was a long list of items he was presumably supposed to have – or avoid. He gave me a chicken leg and poured himself a mugful of blueberries.

Through a blueberry he told me how he had written his lines on a girl's forehead in *Mutiny on the Bounty* because he could not remember them. Then he invited me to have a look at his telephone equipment. He was an amateur radio ham, and when bored he would telephone around the world to chat, not telling them who he was. By great good luck I had met an enthusiastic ham he knew in Patagonia. The equipment stretched the wall of the room, some 30 feet along the side of what turned out to be his bedroom. Then he ushered me on a short trip around a few rooms, and after we had said hello to a boy sitting reading in a chair in the library, the phone rang. Brando turned into a man on the phone who could not get a word in edgeways.

After a few minutes he said he had an appointment, and could he give me a life back to my hotel? So off we went, after he had checked my safety belt was fastened properly. I was being driven round Los Angeles by Marlon Brando! He asked what I had thought when it appeared the Germans were about to invade Britain, I said it had not occurred to us they would have ever succeeded, We drove on – and got lost. He pulled the car into the kerb, pressed a button winding down the window, and asked an old couple if they knew where the hotel I had mentioned was located. They did not, nor did they have any idea whom they were talking to; they turned and slowly walked away. He waited for a long time, watching them, and eventually dropped me off at my hotel. We arranged to meet again.

A telephone call came from his secretary a few days later and I returned to the house. He opened the door, and immediately accused me of smoking. I agreed that I had. In I went again, and this time, for no apparent reason, there were several other people sitting about. There were problems – he had decided to go off on a camping trip with his son. He could not undertake our project. Off they drove, and one of the relieved guests said: 'Thank God he's gone – now we can go out to the pool and have a smoke!' We did.

That was the end of yet another project. I flew to New York, reported to a table of UN officials, and returned to Britain. Several months later my phone rang again. It was Brando once more. He had bought the rights to *Bury My Heart at Wounded Knee* – whom could he talk to in the BBC to make the film? Could he speak to the Director of the BBC? I advised him to contact our New York representative. In the end his offer was politely refused. It had been decided, presumably, that he was too unreliable.

His parting words to me on the phone had been: 'Don't look back! They may be catching up on you!' I'll never know why we met. Perhaps he had just been tormenting the United Nations.

Hugh Burnett

The Whole Royal Family

QUEEN ELIZABETH II came to the throne in 1952, and after 25 years it was decided that the event should be remembered with suitable celebrations. This meant that the poor lady had to go round the suburbs of London, meeting various local dignitaries and receiving their loyal best wishes.

The day was scheduled to close with fireworks on the Thames. The great and the good had been invited to watch these from the top four floors of the Millbank Tower and a splendid champagne supper had been laid on for them there – presumably at tax-payers' expense.

The lower two floors were for very important people; the floor above was for really important people; and the top floor was strictly for royals and prime ministers only.

Someone had decided that the music to accompany the fireworks should be chosen by the fine artist, John Piper. Piper was as vague as he was talented, and the job of giving him technical assistance, as well as a few practical suggestions, went to my wife, Faith. She and Piper made up a short tape comprised of little bits of British music – Handel, Britten, Vaughan Williams, etc – to which the pyrotechnic display would somehow be matched. When the evening arrived, the whole royal family, with the exception of Princess Alexandra – who had been sent to Alexandra

Palace, and would have become Queen if a bomb had destroyed the tower – assembled for the party on the top floor. Faith and I were on this floor too, because it had been decided that we were the only ones who could start the music tape, and thus the firework display, on cue.

The evening did not start well. It was pouring with rain and the clouds were very low. The Queen arrived a little bit later than the others and was whisked straight into the lift. A soon as she arrived at the top, she made a beeline for the Queen Mother, who happened to be standing beside me (and who must have been wondering who on earth I was).

'Where are my dry shoes?' demanded Her Majesty junior.

'I left them in the lobby for you,' replied her Mum. 'They are in a Harrods plastic bag.'

HM jnr turned to her lady-in-waiting. 'Fetch them at once. My feet are soaking wet.'

After a few moments the lady-in-waiting returned with a very nervous-looking detective. 'I am afraid, Ma'am, that we can't get your shoes,' he said.

'WHAT?' A look of thunder crossed the royal brow.

'The lifts have all been sealed as a security measure.' (Yes, thought I, so that all the detectives can have an hour off and enjoy the party 'below stairs'.)

From then on HM was not exactly in a party mood.

Various dignitaries were presented. I chatted lightly, very lightly, with Princesses Margaret and Anne until the time for the fireworks drew near. Then everyone – everyone except the Queen, that is – moved to the windows to watch. Faith went into a special control room and I stood in a doorway from where I could give her signal as soon as the Queen got to her vantage point.

Ah, but majesty doesn't work like that, especially if it happens to be in a bad mood, with wet feet. No courtier murmured in the royal ear. No field marshal waved a gracious, gloved hand in the direction of a red carpet or a gold chair. Was the Queen going to stroll over to an empty window on her own and peer out? She was not. She did not budge an inch. The Prime Minister, Mr Callaghan, to whom she was talking, risked his neck with an interruption. After all, the whole nation was waiting, via the BBC. 'There are fireworks starting now, I believe, Ma'am.'

Her Majesty took no notice whatsoever.

Frantic commentators on radio and television made renewed efforts at small talk as the cameras showed only the barges – silently waiting in the teeming rain.

The heck with it, I thought and gave the signal. Whoosh! Whoosh! The music blared and the rockets shot into the clouds. 'Why don't they blow up the barges?' cried the Duke of Edinburgh, leaping from window to window.

But the Queen never moved a muscle, even though the fireworks were for her.

I expect that she has mellowed a bit, now that she is a gran.

Colin Clark

Chuck Berry

FOR MANY years I commuted between the Essex village where I live and London. One winter evening I boarded my usual train at Liverpool Street station, and on entering the compartment I saw there was a tall, rather distinguished-looking black man with greyish hair sitting in one of the corners, examining the contents of his opened briefcase that he had balanced on his knees. I smiled and nodded and he returned the courtesy.

When I had settled myself in the corner diagonally across from him I noticed a black porter who was progressing down the platform suddenly stop and peer in the window obviously inspecting my fellow passenger. He boarded the train and from the open doorway of our compartment told the black man in the corner that the second class was 'down there' – which he indicated with an outstretched arm and finger.

My fellow passenger looked surprised and puzzled and the porter then asked for his ticket. This was produced with arm outstretched from a sitting position, but the porter in the doorway declined to take it because he said he did not have his reading glasses with him.

I took the proffered ticket and informed the porter that it was a first-class return ticket to Ipswich, whereupon he snorted and withdrew.

My fellow passenger asked me what that was all about, and I noticed his American accent. I pinched the flesh on my cheek and replied: 'You're black – that's what that was about.'

He smiled, shook his head and said, 'It happens all the time.'

I then asked him why he was going to Ipswich. He said he was giving a concert there later that evening, and with a jerk of his head indicated what was obviously a guitar on the luggage rack. I asked him his name and he said he was Chuck Berry.

He could tell by my reaction, or rather lack of one, that I hadn't the remotest idea who Chuck Berry was, but he just smiled and passed over a promotional leaflet for me to read. We had a delightful conversation until I left the train at my station.

When I told my wife, who met me off the train, of my encounter she was speechless at my ignorance. My daughter gave me a Chuck Berry cassette as a Christmas present later that month.

George Winstanley

Brendan Behan

FORTY-TWO YEARS AGO Brendan Behan was in town for the first performance of *The Hostage*. My father, Robert Pitman, book reviewer of the *Sunday Express*, had coped with Brendan before, and was asked by the publishers to chaperone their playwright for the London leg of his tour.

I was eight years old, and my overwhelming preoccupation was Guy Fawkes Night. Behan's impending arrival was very small beer to me. This particular afternoon I sat in my father's office clutching a box of Brock's and Standard's fireworks. My father's secretary told me that Dad would be taking me to the pub to meet 'a very famous gentleman'.

The bar was warm and full of raucous laughter. The catalyst was a stout-ish man dressed in a shabby gaberdine coat, with a beaming red face and a disproportionately small mouth. Feet (also small) were encased in grubby white plimsolls, minus laces. With a glass in one hand, making sweeping gestures with the other, Brendan Behan was holding court, and the place was humming.

He suddenly caught a glimpse of the eight-year-old with the box, and asked my father who I was. He asked me about my fireworks and listened as I detailed the ones with the biggest bang, the most glittering sparkle and so on. Then, from somewhere inside his coat Behan produced a ten-shilling note (a fortune to a small boy in those days), and said, 'Now, Jonathan,

I want you to do something for me. I want you to buy the biggest bloody rocket you can get for this.' Pressing the note into my hand, he added, 'On the condition that when it goes up you shout, at the top of your voice now, "UP THE REPUBLIC!"'

A year later, I read my first 'proper' book, *Kettleby's Zoo* by Peter Ling. My father suggested I should write a little essay about it and, eventually, my piece was printed on his book review page. My parents had hundreds of friends and colleagues, yet not one of them commented on my 'review'. I got paid a couple of guineas, and that was that.

Two weeks later, however, a postcard arrived from Dublin, written in a curious mixture of Irish and English, and addressed to 'My friend Jonathan'. It said how impressive my review was, and what a lovely book it sounded, and told me to keep up the writing.

The man who had taken the trouble to write this, go to the post office, buy a stamp and put the card in the post was very ill, with not long to live. But he remembered the little fella with the box of fireworks, whom he had met so briefly.

Jonathan Pitman

Bette Davis

WHEN I WAS 16 a showbiz pal of mine called George asked me whether I would like to meet Bette Davis. I nearly dropped dead. He knew the lady well and told me that she was staying in London at the Dorchester and that I could see her for ten minutes. 'You can't stay longer,' he said. 'You're not on her schedule.'

The next morning George led me through the hotel, tiptoeing along the deep plush carpets, his head bent in reverence as if we had both been granted an audience with the Pope. We entered a suite and the resplendent figure of Bette Davis turned around in a kind of swirl as if she had been facing a camera crew on a film set. She flung out her arms to my friend and cried in that famous voice, 'Hello!' adding throatily, 'How lo-ve-ly to see you!' Then, as a sort of postscript, she added: 'And this must be your little friend Pa-tr-ick. How nice...' She smoked continuously, puffing and flicking ash everywhere, and with her bulging eyes and peculiar way of fracturing her sentences with pauses, she looked exactly like Baby Jane. True, she wasn't plastered with white make-up, and Joan Crawford wasn't chained to a nearby bed, but she did swish around the room as she talked, all the time aiming sudden glances at me. It was quite alarming.

George then showed her some papers and a script that had to be read. There was also a pile of photographs from fans that needed signing. I watched closely as she read through her mail and wrote her extravagant signature on the photographs. As she wrote she said to me loudly: 'Of course, you know I've never thought of myself as being famous at all. But when you go to an Oscar ceremony, as I have done, and you get the reception that I get, then you feel very honoured. Did you know that Hollywood is the only place outside Britain that has royalty? Royalty is motion picture people. You see, Americans think of us as kings and queens. It's like your royalty – it must never ev-er go. Millions of darling little people ne-ed us.'

With that she was finished and it was time for us to go. George gave her a kiss on the cheek and said he would ring later. She shook my hand limply, saying, 'It was lo-ve-ly to meet you, dear.' I realised then she was off her trolley.

Twenty years later I met her again, in Hatchard's bookshop in Piccadilly. The manager of the shop knew that another pal of mine was a whizzkid photographer. La Davis was in town to sign copies of her autobiography and he wanted some shots of her in the shop. Come the day, Whizzkid and I walked down Piccadilly and I stopped and stared. Whizzkid gasped. From the door of Hatchard's all the way along to Green Park stretched a queue, four deep, of thousands of people waiting to see Bette Davis.

A rather nervous sales lady, after checking our credentials and letting us through the doors, said, 'Nothing like this has ever happened here. The most we've had for a signing session was for Pam Ayres.'

Moments later there was a cheer from the crowd outside and a giant limousine purred into view. The car door opened and the mob surged forward. Out stepped a tiny wizened figure who looked little more than four foot tall. She was dressed in black with a bizarre hat that looked like a crown – a Rumpelstiltskin figure bent over almost double.

As she tottered into the shop she gave a sideways glance at the heaving crowd. I caught a glimpse of her eyes as she stared at the fans. It was terrifying. The manager introduced Whizzkid and myself to her and she proffered me a gloved hand. I mentioned that we had met many years before. She attempted a cracked smile and said, 'How lo-ve-ly,' in a splendidly insincere way. Whizzkid looked speechless.

She made her way to an enormous table, where there was a huge pile of books. The manager asked her if she would like a drink, 'to refresh you after your journey' (she had come all of two minutes away from Park Lane), and she snapped, 'I'll have a large vodka – and I mean large.' Within minutes a tray had appeared complete with a large glass of vodka. 'Th-ank you,' she said, throwing her head back and gulping from the glass. She immediately asked for another and then shouted, 'Now, let's get down to work! Let the people in!' A stampede followed, and Whizzkid kept taking pictures, watching all the time with morbid fascination.

Looking back, you had to hand it to the lady. As the day wore on she refused to take a break from signing, merely ordering more vodka. Her signature got wobblier by the minute. By closing time it was undecipherable. The manager closed the doors and the staff looked exhausted. But not la Davis. She suddenly looked at me triumphantly and shouted: 'You there! I did my job today and that's why I've lasted in this business. They don't come bigger than me!'

Still off her trolley, I thought. Never mind, she'd signed over 1,000 books – which is more than you could say for Pam Ayres.

Patrick Newley

Jorge Luis Borges

IT WAS AN ESPECIALLY cold January, I think in 1963. I was working as a guide for the British Council in London. My assignment for this particular day was to take an eminent Argentinian writer to three houses in Sussex and Kent with literary vibrations. We were to have a car with a driver.

He was travelling with his mother, Leonora Acevedo de Borges, a small woman in a velvet hat and enormous fur coat, her clear, direct eyes missing nothing. He was not very tall and wore thick glasses, through which I think he could only see shadows. There was a calm smile on his face and he had a soft handshake. He, too, wore an enormous overcoat.

The snow was thick on the pavements before we left London. By the time we got to the lane that led to Bateman's, the home of Rudyard Kipling, it was clear that it was completely impassable. We then made for Rye, to see Lamb House, where Henry James had lived for so long, only to find that it was never open on that day of the week and certainly not in winter. Someone at headquarters had blundered.

We had an excellent lunch at the Mermaid Hotel.

He called his mother Mama, with the accent on the first syllable, and she called him Jorge. Having heard radio announcers tying their glottises in knots in order to say 'Horche Lueeth Borcheth', I asked her how to pronounce his name correctly. 'Jorge Luis Borges,' she replied, exactly as it is written, the g's and j's very soft, the s's sibilant.

Our third appointment was at the house of H G Wells in Sandgate, near Folkestone, and here we were expected. It was a house in the style of C F A Voysey, probably even by him. Our hostess, wearing a dirndl skirt and sandals with no stockings, welcomed us into a stone-flagged hall even colder than outside. She gave us tea in that hall, glancing disapprovingly at Mama's neat suede boots and huge fur coat – which she did not remove – explaining that her sandals were made of plastic and that she was entirely vegetarian. She gave us scones made of stone-ground flour, the proportion of stone to flour approximately equal.

He said very little over tea, a Buddhist smile on his face, enjoying the brittle conversation of the woman. Only in England, he said to me later, did people like that flourish unhindered. HG Wells still haunted the house, we were told. No woman could have a bath in the housemaids' bathroom on the top floor, because H G came in and stared at them, sitting on the lavatory seat with the lid down.

As we prepared to leave he said to me:

'Are we near Canterbury?'

'Yes,' I said.

'Have we time to go?'

He had had a disappointing day. They were not usually very pleased at headquarters when programmes were altered or interfered with, but he obviously wanted to go very much. Fortunately, our driver was one of the more amenable of a very recalcitrant lot.

It was dark when we arrived and evensong was being sung in the choir. The nave was only partially lit, and I heard Mama catch her breath as we entered. 'Unbelievable,' she said. We sat in the ambulatory behind the choir; as the service continued, the treble and bass voices seemed to reflect the light and shadow of the ceiling arches.

He touched me on the sleeve.

'I want to go back to the nave,' he said.

Together we went down that wide flight of perfectly plain steps until we stood at the bottom.

'Am I in the middle?'

We moved.

'Am I facing the altar?'

I manoeuvred him slightly and he said:

'Now you must face me.'

I did so, my back to the choir.

'And now,' he said, 'I fulfil a lifelong ambition. I am here in Canterbury Cathedral and I am going to recite you the Lord's Prayer in Anglo-Saxon.'

A beatific smile spread slowly over his face and seemed to envelop his entire person.

Only then did he do so.

Laurence Fleming

Douglas Bader

THE YEAR was 1982, and Sir Douglas Bader was to be interviewed by Michael Parkinson. A young researcher was sent to talk to him in his mews house near the Albert Hall. Within half-an-hour Sir Douglas phoned to say he was sending her back as she knew nothing about him. I was asked to go in her place. 'Do you mind?' the producer asked. Mind! I'd have paid for the privilege.

I knew all about him, of course. A biography had just been written by his friend 'Laddie' Lucas and I asked for an hour or two to skim through it. Somehow, I managed to grasp the fundamentals of Bader's views on how the Battle of Britain should have been fought, what the Duxford Wing was, why there were differences of opinion between 11 and 12 Fighter Groups, pilot shortage and Lord Dowding's strengths and weaknesses.

Nevertheless it was not without trepidation that I rang his doorbell. My hero opened the door and beamed. 'Thank God they didn't send a young researcher.' I laughed. 'Come in, my dear. I can only give you 45 minutes because I have to pick up the old duck.' I daringly asked who that was. 'My wife, Joan. And God help me if I'm late.'

I asked him if he'd be able to come down the steps leading to the TV interview area. 'No problem, my dear. If I fall down, Parky can come and pick me up. That'll be a laugh to start with.'

He said he only had a problem with his legs if he had to kneel. When he went to receive his knighthood, 'old' Dicky Gillette (everybody was referred to as 'old' this or that) worried in case he overbalanced and decided they'd better have a rehearsal. 'Good idea, old boy,' Douglas had said. 'Don't want me falling down flat on my face and bringing HER down, do we?' Fortunately 'old' Johnny Mills and another chum, 'old' Neil Cameron, were also there. They both pretended they had tin legs, and fell about all over the place. Altogether they had 'a good giggle'. I soon discovered that Sir Douglas's main aim in life was to have a good giggle.

Sir Douglas didn't want to talk about flying, the Battle of Britain, or being a PoW. 'Oh forget about that. Everybody knows about it. They've seen the film and think I'm Kenneth Moore.' He laughed uproariously.

We talked about sport, and the joy of still being able to compete, with or without legs. He was full of admiration for the chaps who played wheelchair basketball. He nearly fell off his chair with laughter recalling a game he'd watched in Canada. The referee was unpopular, so the participants ran him down and he had to be carried off.

His philosophy regarding loss of limbs was that the younger you lost them the better! He meant that it is much easier to adapt when young. He was tremendously enthusiastic about the work he did talking to other disabled people.

Inevitably the conversation came round to golf. He'd had one of his artificial limbs shortened to improve his stroke and hit the ball much further. 'Old Henry Longhurst could never understand the principle of this. Said I'd had the wrong leg shortened. Ha, Ha, Ha.'

He secretly enjoyed a spot of fortune-telling. A couple of years later he and his wife Joan went to a fete near Banbury. Noticing a booth marked 'Fortune Teller', he popped in. The lady inside said she wasn't really a fortune-teller but was in touch with 'the other side'. She told him, 'Someone called Henry wants to tell you that he went to sleep for a little while and then woke up. He's now doing exactly as he wants, and he'd like you to know that the grass is a great deal greener this side than it ever was over your side.' Douglas was adamant Henry had sent a promised message.

Douglas often went to Scotland to play golf with his good friend, Jan Collins, the publisher. Jan always arranged for Douglas to have one particular caddie, Andy Anderson, a dour Scotsmen. 'He's long since gone up there to join Henry, where the fairways are greener. Ha, Ha, Ha, Ha!' One day, as they were completing a round of golf at Troon, Jan told him about a lovely course called Machrihanish, over the water on the Mull of Kintyre. 'Let's go over,' said Douglas. 'I've got my aeroplane at Prestwick. It'll only take us 20 minutes to fly.' As they finished the game, he said to Andy, 'I'll pick you up in the morning in my car, drive you to Prestwick and we'll fly over there.' Andy stopped dead in his tracks, and banged Douglas's bag of clubs onto the ground with a determined thump. 'I'll no fly with ye, ye mad bugger,' he said, and they never did play Machrihanish.

Andy's description of Douglas prompted me to say that I'd heard his language when flying was very colourful, and that the RT had to be turned off so that the WAAF in the ops room couldn't hear him. 'Nonsense,' he said. 'I can't remember saying anything worse than "My eyes are hanging out like dog's balls, and I can't see a bloody thing". The girls loved it. Ha, Ha, Ha, Ha.'

I asked him whether he thought youngsters today would be prepared to fight and die for this country, as he and all his contemporaries had been. 'Of course they would. People don't change. The country doesn't change. Our parents thought we were a bunch of bums in our wide trousers with long scarves wrapped round our necks.'

I wonder. Had he lived long enough to see Channel 4's *Secret Lives*, would he have defended the odious youngsters who made it? Hopefully he would have had an opportunity to 'shoot them down in flames, old boy'.

All the time we'd been talking, Sir Douglas had been lighting his pipe, puffing it, knocking it out, or re-filling it. Suddenly he knocked it out again, without re-filling it. There was a certain finality about it. My 45 minutes had gone in a flash.

'Well there you are, my dear! Can I give you a lift anywhere?' he asked. 'I'm going to Hyde Park Corner.' I was going in the opposite direction. 'Oh thank you,' I said. 'Hyde Park Corner will be wonderful.' Anything for a few minutes with my hero.

I asked if I could use his bathroom. 'Yes, but hurry. I daren't be late for the old duck.' I'd hardly got up the stairs when I heard him revving up.

'Bang the door behind you and leap in,' he said, the Mini already on the move. The mews became a runway, and I was in a Spitfire, taking off down the narrow cobbled lane. He darted between cars on Kensington Gore – I swear we were airborne. We screamed to a halt just in time, as Lady Bader walked up from the other direction. She took my place, and the Spitfire zoomed away.

He'd told me that, during the war, he'd been able to park his aeroplane outside his hut – no running out to it like you see on the films. So I arranged for him to park his Mini right outside TV Centre, for the programme. Vera Lynn was one of the other guests, and sang 'We'll Meet Again'. When Sir Douglas was ready to leave. I took him down to his car. He gave me a kiss and said 'We will meet again, Eve.' I was thrilled, although I couldn't quite see how. A few weeks later he died. Now it will have to be on the other side, where the grass is greener.

Eve Lucas

Charlie Chaplin

IT WAS the early 1970s, and I was an 11-year-old prep schoolboy in London for half-term. My father kept an attic room in Albany as an occasional pad, and on high days and holidays we would all sleep in this eyrie – 72 stone stairs up and no lift, with a communal bathroom down the corridor. I loved it.

On this particular morning my father and I strolled down Albany's rope-walk into the courtyard where I was to meet my best friend and his father for a day of London treats. We were lurking on the corner by Meakers – a gentle-men's outfitters opposite Fortnum & Mason – when suddenly, as if stung by a bee, my father left my side and darted through the throbbing traffic to the other side of Piccadilly. This unnerved me, because given his age he was not much given to darting.

I lost sight of him among the shoppers thronging the pavement and began to panic. Should I cross over and look for him and risk missing my school chum, or should I stay put and risk losing my father? Anxiously, I scanned the other side of the street as far as I was able between the bustling taxis and buses, but he was completely lost to view. Then the traffic cleared, and I saw him out-side Hatchard's, approaching a distinguished-looking gentleman who was ap-parently absorbed in one of the bookshop's windows. The man raised his hat – which I seem to remember was a black homburg – and shook hands with my pa. Presently my father pointed across Piccadilly and both men looked in my direction; my father – who had a remarkable facility for embarrassing me in public – then bellowed my name several times and beckoned furiously for me to join them.

I was torn; the shyness of an only child made me hate meeting my father's friends, whose self-assured urbanity and well-meaning breeziness served only to highlight my gaucherie and tongue-tied responses, but this was outweighed by my very urgent desire to get my father to stop shouting my name at the top of his voice across the width of Piccadilly. Blushing horribly, I ran across the street towards my tormenting parent. Smiling sweetly, I looked up at his companion, who raised the homburg to me as my father said: 'Mr Chaplin, may I introduce my son Jonathan? Jonathan, meet Mr Charles Chaplin.'

I was nonplussed. Of course I had heard of Charlie Chaplin – who hadn't? – but he was a scruffy character with an ill-fitting bowler, a small moustache, a cane and bandy legs. I sensed a joke that I hadn't quite grasped – my father was always a bit of a tease – and I giggled in what I took to be a polite and non-committal way. Mr Chaplin shook my hand, told me that he was delighted to meet me and hoped that I was well, whereupon he turned and expressed similar pleasure at having made my father's acquaintance, doffed his hat to us both and slipped away past Fortnum's and down Duke Street.

I gasped at my father: 'Who was that?' 'Charlie Chaplin,' he replied. I was still unconvinced. 'How do you know him?' I demanded. 'I don't,' said my father. 'I recognised him across the street and introduced myself, thinking what a treat it would be for you to be able to say that you had met Charlie Chaplin.'

Despite the embarrassment he had caused me I remember being filled with affection for my father for having done what he did. And if he said that it was Charlie Chaplin then that was good enough for me. We crossed back to the north side of Piccadilly and met my friend Stephen and his father. As soon as we were alone I blurted out to Stephen my adventure, but he didn't believe a word of it. 'Don't be silly. Charlie Chaplin had a bowler hat, a moustache and bandy legs. Anyway, he's been dead for years.' (In fact he did not die until 1977.)

I was miserable. We spent the day arguing over whether I was a liar or just plain stupid. To make it worse, once back at school after half-term no one there believed me either. Perhaps this was my penance for always having preferred Laurel and Hardy.

Jonathan Ray

Sally Mugabe

THE NAME MUGABE is not sweet music in the ears of many people but I have a reason to be thankful to one who carried that name.

In the early Sixties I was a young magistrate in Rhodesia. Robert Mugabe was in political detention, and there was considerable unrest in the country, including a peaceful protest by the womenfolk of political detainees and their sympathisers outside the parliament building in Salisbury. Though merely a sit-down in the roadway, unaccompanied by any violence, it was nevertheless an unlawful assembly.

The police arrested the protestors, who numbered, with their children, some 500. Since it was necessary to remand most of them to a future date, they were detained in a special section of the prison, consisting of a large courtyard. The maximum period for a remand was 14 days, at the end of which very few women had been tried. They were not readily co-operating in the judicial process, and it was necessary to have another round of re-manding the accused. The chief magistrate called a meeting to discuss ways of dealing with this problem.

The standard method of remanding the women would be to transport them in batches of ten or so to the court, explain that they could not be tried immediately, remand them in custody for another 14 days, and transport them back to the prison. This would take several days and occupy the time of several magistrates, to the disadvantage of other prisoners awaiting trial.

Being young and enthusiastic, I told the meeting that the law did not require the women to be brought to court. The magistrates court was where the magistrate chooses to sit – or, in this case, stand. Nor was it necessary to remand the ladies in batches. All that the law required was that the order of remand be pronounced in their presence after giving them the opportunity to be heard. Instead of the women being brought to the magistrate, the magistrate should be brought to the prisoners, and they could be remanded *en masse*.

The chief magistrate seemed impressed, but he wore an odd sort of smile. He said that I, as the father of this original idea, should also be the midwife.

I travelled to the prison the next day. One of the warders unlocked the iron door to the women's courtyard. With all the ignorance amassed over 25 years I marched into the centre of the courtyard – and the massed women.

I explained our difficulties to the ladies, and my proposed solution.

Unlike the chief magistrate, they were unimpressed with my brilliance. From where they had been sitting in groups, quietly nursing their children and chatting, they rose to their feet as one and began to advance towards me, ululating with that soft but menacing sound that only black women seem to be able to produce. Their intent was clear even to me. The leading women were already clawing at my clothing and body, and I was in danger of falling under the weight of bodies, when a tall, elegant woman made herself heard above the chilling ululation.

I did not know it at the time, but she was Sally Mugabe, Robert Mugabe's wife. A Ghanaian, a selfless and dedicated revolutionary and a woman of great presence, she spoke to her fellow detainees. They stopped their advance and listened. She spoke in Chisona, the local language, of which I understood a little. What she said was unflattering, but I was happy to hear it. She said they should not vent their anger upon me: I was a mere lickspittle of Ian Smith, unworthy of their revolutionary ire, and they should save their energies for the real battle to come. Warily I made my way through the press of women to the courtyard door. Once I was tripped and kicked, but I reached safety uninjured.

I realised from the expression on those women's faces that, but for Sally Mugabe, I would not have survived that day. She herself survived the revolution, became first lady of Zimbabwe and did much good for women and children in that now sad country. She died in 1992. Her death coincided with the beginning of Robert Mugabe's descent from moderately responsible leadership to insanity.

James Findu

Herbert von Karajan

IN THE AUTUMN of 1954 I was appointed assistant porter with the Philharmonic Orchestra, then under the baton of the Austrian maestro Herbert von Karajan. An orchestra of 100-plus players uses around two tons of instruments, and their transportation on a major concert tour presents a formidable exercise in logistics. My job was to deal with any problems at customs or with theatre managements at such venues as La Scala in Milan, the Tonhalle in Zurich and l'Opéra in Paris.

En route to our first concert in the Festspielhaus in Antwerp, customs at Ostend insisted on opening the coffin-like containers containing the double basses and checking them against the manifest. Eventually we were let through and boarded a bus for Antwerp. There was no time to go to our hotel, so the orchestra had to change into formal attire in cramped and awkward conditions, which put them in a very bad mood.

Karajan, who had arrived more than an hour earlier in his bright-red Ferrari roadster, was pacing impatiently up and down while his valet, Guido, and the orchestra's founder and artistic director, Walter Legge, who discovered and married the great soprano Elisabeth Schwarzkopf, tried to soothe him. As soon as we arrived, he launched into one of his gruelling rehearsals, at the end of which there was just enough time for the musicians to gulp down some coffee and a brioche before the concert started at 8pm.

The programme was to begin with Cherubini's overture to *Anacreonte*, followed by Benjamin Britten's *Variations on a Theme by Frank Bridge* and Tchaikovsky's Fifth, with the overture to Verdi's *La Forza del Destino* as the encore.

The musicians, including the late, great horn virtuoso Dennis Brain, were in a rebellious mood. Clem Relph, the librarian, had put all the music on the stands, but a deputation told him the orchestra would not play the Verdi. 'You tell that Austrian sergeant-major that we are bloody tired and we want to eat before midnight, so no Verdi,' warned a spokesman from the percussion section, usually the bolshiest group in the orchestra.

Clem said he would pass the message on but, understandably, did no such thing. The orchestra played magnificently. Deafening applause greeted the overture, and there was a five-minute standing ovation for the Tchaikovsky with the audience screaming '*Bis! Bis!*' Karajan took several bows and came into the wings, where he whipped off his tails, under which he wore only a dicky. Guido mopped the Maestro's perspiring lean frame with a luxurious Turkish towel and gave him a fresh tailcoat, while Karajan brushed his silvery blue hair into place.

The audience were stamping their feet and calling for more. Karajan took yet another bow. As he did so, he muttered through the corner of his mouth to the leader, Manoug Parikian, 'We shall now play *La Forza*.' Parikian, who was in league with the rest of the orchestra, looked at Karajan impassively. 'We cannot,' he said. 'The music has not been put out.'

Karajan continued to acknowledge the huge tide of applause with open arms, but the smile on his face had turned decidedly glassy and there was menace in his jade-green, hooded eyes. Once more he strode off the stage while the audience continued to stamp and clap. He stormed into the wings shouting, 'There is no music! There is no music!'

'You didn't forget to put the music out, Clem?' Legge asked.

'No, I bloody well did not,' Clem retorted angrily. 'That lot is just trying it on.' Karajan was beside himself with fury. At this point I said to him in Italian: 'Maestro, the music has been put out, I swear – *lo giuro, lo giuro*.'

'Just go out there and call their bluff,' Legge urged him. 'They'll play.'

The Maestro hesitated and then, like a lion-tamer, he strode out to thunderous applause. A hush descended on the audience as he picked up his baton and held it aloft. He glared at the orchestra and they glared back. They were clutching their instruments in a manner which indicated they were not going to play. Karajan brought the baton down, a gesture that lasted a mere instant. There was a terrible moment when we did not know whether the orchestra would come to heel. But just as the baton reached the end of its downward stroke, violins and violas were swiftly thrust against chins, cellos and double basses were seized, and the rest of the orchestra joined in.

Karajan seemed unsure of my precise function and he always spoke to me in Italian. During rehearsals at La Scala, the percussion was drowning the woodwinds and he asked for the timpani to be moved away from centre stage to the left. This did not please Jim Bradshaw, a crusty Yorkshireman, who argued with him just as he used to argue with Sir Thomas Beecham at the Royal Philharmonic. Karajan turned to me for my opinion. '*Che ne pensa?*'

Jim was furious. 'What are you asking him for?' he demanded. 'He's only a f***ing porter!'

Karajan either did not hear or did not understand this sally, but waited for my answer. I had to say something. I did not want to upset Jim but neither did I want to contradict one of the world's greatest conductors. So I compromised. '*Si, maestro, ma solo un pochino,*' I said. And for Jim's benefit, 'Only a tiny little bit.'

Jim moved his timps a token two inches to the left and everyone, including Karajan, seemed pleased with the outcome. But at that night's performance Jim put the timps very much back in the centre of the stage.

Peter Muccini

Lord Reith

THE OCCASION was the opening of a new factory in East Africa in the late Fifties. This had been developed by the Commonwealth Development Corporation of which, at that time, Lord Reith was the Chairman. He was not personally opening the factory. This was being done by the Governor of the Territory.

As I was in charge of the opening arrangements I met him at the airport where he was arriving by private plane. How he got into that little aircraft I don't know, but he surely had an awful job of getting out, this huge gaunt figure with a formidable face – a face almost of doom and menace with its large hooked nose, downturned mouth, and above all its sunken scar high on his left cheek. I was very nervous having heard much of his reputation of management by fear. Looking at him one could imagine him preaching Hellfire and Brimstone from a Presbyterian pulpit for an hour or two on a Sunday morning in Scotland.

The journey from the airport to the company guest house where he was staying was largely conducted in silence apart except for the occasional groan presumably indicating pain in his cramped limbs. On arrival he insisted on examining every aspect of the guest house. The bedroom first. 'I presume that bed is at least seven foot long,' he said. 'You surely must have been informed that I must have a special bed.'

'Well yes, Sir,' I replied. 'But I was totally unable to get one in this rather underdeveloped country so I put in a double bed hoping that it would be satisfactory if you slept diagonally across it.'

'Are you sure you've got the geometry of this correct?' he grudgingly growled.

The bathroom next. 'That mirror above the basin, it's been set up for a dwarf. I can't possibly shave if I can't see my face. Get it hung another two feet higher immediately.'

Then the sitting room. Much to my relief at this point the wife of one of the directors appeared – a well-appointed, nearly middle-aged female of considerable charm. The atmosphere changed immediately. His Lordship positively enthused over her and as the sun was down ordered me to produce drinks for us all. She had whisky and I said to him I had fresh orange or fresh lime or tonic water. 'What do you mean?' he said. 'I'll have whisky with a little water.' I was a little taken aback as I had been informed he was teetotal. So I poured him a little whisky, gave it to him and proffered the water jug.

'What do you call this?' he said. 'Give me a proper whisky.'

An hour later the best part of the bottle had gone. And so we left him to have his shower as there was a reception in the club for him to meet the staff. His parting shot to me was: 'When meeting the staff I must have a glass of orange juice in my hand. I will not be seen in public drinking alcohol.' A neat piece of hypocrisy if there ever was one.

The next morning when the factory opening was about halfway through I decided to go to the club to see if the celebratory lunch arrangements were in order. I was looking at the name cards on the top table and was infuriated to see that they had all been altered. Who on earth had done that? Suddenly I knew. At the back of the dining room, astonishingly, there emerged from the clearly marked ladies' lavatory door this gaunt frightening figure.

'Leburn!' he roared. 'Do you realise there is only one towel in the ladies' lavatory?'

I was speechless. Later my thought was, only, if only, there had been a lady in the lavatory.

Mike Leburn

Jack Hobbs

I DON'T KNOW if I was ever wheeled into Lord's or the Oval in my pram, but I cannot remember a time when I was not taken to cricket matches. I watched Larwood bowl and Bradman bat, and I saw Chapman lead out his team, wearing a silk shirt which billowed in the breeze, and blue socks.

When choosing a school for me, my father's priorities were cricket and Latin, probably in that order. Patsy Hendren was our coach at one time, but Hobbs was my hero. He must have been in his late forties by the time I first saw him, but he could still play any stroke on any wicket with consummate artistry and grace. His perfect partner was Sutcliffe, with whom he used to sneak such witty singles that the spectators laughed as well as applauded. But this was not all. His combination of mastery and modesty was unique. His goodness shone out almost visibly like an aureole around him: as John Arlott said, 'If he had never scored a run or excelled at any sport, those who knew him must have seen him as a great man, because of the unmistakable nobility of his character.'

He retired while I was still only a schoolgirl, but his performances remained etched on my memory, and every subsequent batsman whom I saw was weighed in the balance and found wanting. I was not an autograph-hunter, and I never tried to waylay him as he left the pavilion. But now you must imagine one of those film clichés in which the pages of a calendar are rapidly turned, or trees bud and instantly shed their leaves, to indicate the passage of time. Cut to 1963.

I was waiting in a queue at Hove Post Office one day when I became aware of a tall, lean old man in a long, dark overcoat standing just in front of me. The counter-clerk was checking the number of words in a telegram, and when he said, 'That comes to nine pounds, sir', the old man exclaimed, 'I say, that's rather a lot, isn't it?' 'Well, let's see if we can cut it down a bit', suggested the clerk; and he proceeded to read aloud the text of the message, expertly translating it into telegramese. In this way, I learned that its purpose was to congratulate the MCC team, who had achieved a notable victory in New Zealand.

I knew that Hobbs in his retirement lived in a flat overlooking the Hove cricket ground, and a sly peep at the old man's profile assured me that it was indeed he. 'How's that, sir? I've got it down to six pounds ten,' said the clerk triumphantly. I followed Hobbs to the door, my own errand forgotten. 'Oh, Sir Jack,' I burbled like a starstruck teenager, 'I'm so glad to have this opportunity of telling you that you've given me more pleasure in my life than anyone except John Gielgud!' (My husband was not there to overhear this.) A tear trickled down the old man's cheek. 'Thank you,' he said with a gentle smile. 'They were great days.'

A few months later, he was dead. He had nursed his wife through a long illness, and when she died he was like the subject of Henry Wotton's verse:

> *She first deceased. He for a little tried*
> *To live without her: liked it not, and died.*

Winefride Pruden

Henry Moore

ONE OF THE perks of my job as Assistant Story Editor in a Soho film company was that my boss Harold would occasionally take me to a theatrical first night – largely, I suspected, as an unspoken bribe for not laughing out loud at his expenses claims.

There was much excitement in 1973 about *Jumpers*, Tom Stoppard's forthcoming new play at the National, to follow his hit *Rosencrantz and Guildenstern Are Dead*, and I was delighted when Harold offered to take me to the opening. It was unmistakably An Event, and the foyer was crammed with glitterati, networking tirelessly and swooping on each other with bird-like cries of recognition and affection. It hummed with social aplomb, and I stood back slightly, happily observing the great and the good at play. I was part of a group of chatterers centred on Sir Michael Balcon, and could see that everyone apart from me was either famous or important, or both, so when a small, ruddy-faced white-haired man appeared beside me I felt a certain solidarity with him. He was obviously no-one either; I thought he might be the gardener, invited, like me, as a token of gratitude or obligation. He was certainly not dressed to kill (I seem to remember a Viyella checked shirt) and had a faint air of having left his wellingtons at the door.

We chatted idly for a while, until Sir Michael suddenly caught sight of him and said, warmly, 'Henry!' and my new friend replied equally warmly, 'Mick!'

Sir Michael introduced the group by gesturing vaguely at everyone, naming us all and ending with 'and this is Henry Moore', after which he turned back to his friends and ignored him.

To tide over what seemed something of a slight, I said, sympathetically, 'It must be awful being called Henry Moore.' 'Oh really,' he said with interest. 'And why would that be?' 'Well, you know,' I explained helpfully, 'people might think you're the Henry Moore, the famous one – you know, big things with holes.' 'Well, there's always that chance, I suppose,' he replied, giving me a wistful smile. At that point the group shifted slightly and, with a wave, he disappeared into the crowd.

As he left, Michael Balcon turned to me, and as he began to speak, I began to feel slightly sick. 'What an astonishing man. So delightful, so unpretentious. You would never think, would you, that he had set the art world by its ears...'

I can't say I remember much about the play.

Flora Hinton

Hermione Gingold

I FIRST ENCOUNTERED Hermione Gingold forty years ago, when I was acting, writing and directing for Stephen Joseph's Scarborough theatre in the round. She was installed in a front bedroom in his house overlooking the bay. The house had at one time been a vicarage – Alan Ayckbourn lives there now – and with its fifteen rooms it made an ideal HQ from which to run a theatre. During the summer season it was filled with actors, directors, agents and writers, but a bed always seemed to be available when required. Luxury was not guaranteed, but such comforts as were available were bestowed on Hermione. At least she had a large bed.

'Absolutely essential,' Stephen explained. 'She uses her bed as a filing cabinet.' The full extent of this was revealed when the daily help took advantage of a temporary absence to make the bed.

Not only did a quantity of correspondence come to light, but a variety of other articles, including library books and a radio. Miss Gingold was not amused. She declared she would never be able to find anything again.

When I accompanied her on walks, the shortest, most prosaic stroll became charged with the quality of a number from a Gingold revue. Pausing on the promenade, exposed to the blast of a northerly gale, her voice carried for a hundred yards. 'Ooooh! This wind is blowing my eyelashes off.'

She was recognised immediately in Scarborough's largest department store. We were taking a shortcut through the carpet department when she paused and pointed dramatically. She couldn't point any other way, for even a simple gesture was conditioned by years on stage to achieve the maximum effect. 'Look!' she commanded. High above the rolls of Wilton and Axminster were displayed rugs, cunningly woven from raffia or rushes to resemble animal skins – tiger and zebra lookalikes. That one word was enough to set shop assistants running. The rugs had been hung up beyond human reach (presumably the store was not expecting a brisk sale) but a ladder was soon fetched and an assistant swarmed up it. Twice. Once for the raffia tiger and once again for the woven zebra. The trophies were laid reverently at Hermione's feet. 'Fascinating,' she breathed; and one could almost see the young man calculating the commission on his sale. 'Yes, indeed...' Pause. 'I have one just like it in my bedroom at home.' With a nod of approval she swept on and away to the grocery department.

I must accept some of the blame for what happened there. I have always been fond of my food and, having discovered one of the best provision stores in the North Riding, I felt a proprietorial pride in showing it off. The shop had recently switched to self-service, so we were able to wander through avenues of temptingly arrayed goodies. Sharing my interest in gastronomic delights, my companion began to fill a trolley. Tins, packets and jars mounted up. Were those actually plovers' eggs? Products from far corners of the world were gathered into the basket. They made an extravagant pile and the mind boggled at the probable bill as the load was trundled towards the checkout. A reverential hush prevailed as the girl at the cash register prepared to tot up the windfall of the week. But at the brink Miss Gingold paused again.

'I must be mad,' she remarked in ringing tones. 'I can get all this in Harrods.' And after a quick about-turn returned every item to its place on the shelf.

Hermione had her own ideas on cooking. Her particular speciality had evolved from years of catering for young actors and students who had developed a homing instinct towards her door.

She explained that such a dish needed to be tasty, economical, simple to prepare and capable of being made in vast quantities. The ingredients were straightforward. Marmalade, a spoonful at a time, was stirred into a saucepan of baked beans and tasted until the desired richness had been achieved. Frankfurters were added, cut into inch-long pieces; the whole was heated gently, then kept hot until required. It may sound elementary, but the recipe actually worked. At least it did on the evening when Hermione prepared supper with her own hands for a party of Stephen's students.

Years passed. We met again after the first night of a West End play in which she had starred. I seldom visit dressing-rooms because I never know what to say. On this occasion I had my opening line ready – the conventional 'You won't remember me, but...' Her tiny room was full of flowers and people, with more arriving all the time. I began to have doubts. What was I doing breathing down Robert Helpmann's neck in a crowd of celebrities? I would have turned and fled, but the pressure from behind forced me to shuffle on. Then we were face to face: whereupon she rendered me dumb by taking the words out of my mouth.

'I remember you,' she said.

David Campton

Peter Cook

MY PARENTS were delighted with their new handyman. 'He's really very good,' my mother phoned to tell me. 'He's put up some lovely shelves in the study and is painting the garden chairs. He's called Mr Cook.'

Cambridge in 1975 was in a state of controlled panic. A rapist was at large, and single women were warned to keep their doors and windows locked at night. He was known to be short and stocky, and apparently wore black leather and a mask with the word RAPIST written across it. He was both sexually and verbally violent, and left his victims in a state of physical and psychological terror.

The police seemed incapable of tracing him, although they made a practice of re-arresting and then releasing several likely suspects, among them Mr Cook. My mother, kind-hearted and unworldly, was outraged on his behalf, and listened with sympathy to his grievances. 'It's just because I'm a little feller,' he would complain with wounded innocence. 'They've got it in for me.' She would make another cup of tea, and nod encouragingly.

'I feel so sorry for him,' she told me. 'He's never had much of a chance in life, and just because he has a criminal record – only burglary, when he was much younger! – they keep on questioning him. He's made a new start, and they keep raking it up.' His being taken in for questioning happened so frequently that my brother, still living at home, used to greet him jocularly with, 'Hello, not caught you yet, I see'. This was met with a mirthless laugh.

Unprepossessing though he was, he had acquired a wife who, I was told, was devoted to him. Their sadness was that they were childless, so when my sister came over from Montreal for the summer with her two young children, it seemed a delightful idea for him and his wife to take them punting – after all, he worked in the boatyard; what could be more suitable?

A picnic was prepared, and off they went. My six-year-old nephew fell into the Cam and was heroically rescued by Mr Cook, and his popularity in my parents' household was never higher.

Some weeks later, I went home for the weekend. The rapes had increased in number and brutality, but I was blithely confident that these at least had happened on dark evenings in halls of residence, and this was a Saturday in broad daylight. Nonetheless, my parents warned me, as they went out for the afternoon, not to open the door to just anyone, so when the doorbell rang I opened it very cautiously.

There stood a short, stocky, shifty-looking man – it must be Mr Cook! And indeed it was. 'Thank goodness it's you,' I said hospitably, ushering him in. 'I was afraid it might be the rapist!'

Our eyes met briefly; his expression was impassive. 'Well, you can never be too careful. Are your parents in?' On learning that I was on my own, he hesitated for a while. Then he pushed past me quite roughly, saying that he wanted to check the shelves he had put up last week. Halfway down the hall, he abruptly turned round and said he had changed his mind. 'I just want to know how satisfied they were with the drawer I repaired on that military chest,' he said. 'I've done a lovely job on it – let me show you, it's in the top bedroom.'

'What about the shelves you wanted to check on?'

'No, it's the drawer,' he insisted.

I was beginning to feel uneasy, but after all, this was someone who had saved my nephew's life! Just then the phone rang, and when I returned he had gone. Three days later my mother rang me at six in the morning. 'Flora!' she almost squeaked. 'It's on the news – they've caught the rapist! And it's Mr Cook!' She was so shaken that, although almost teetotal, she agreed to have a small brandy. My brother was frankly disbelieving.

'A mask with RAPIST on it?' he scoffed. 'He surely doesn't have the imagination.' But it seemed that he did. Once he was in custody, hindsight illuminated all corners and opprobrium was cast from all directions, but my mother, fair-minded as always, wrote to the highest authorities and – on the grounds that a man is innocent until proven guilty – wanted it on file that Mr Cook had been a good worker and furthermore had saved her grandson from a watery grave. But by this time, Peter Cook was in a hospital for the criminally insane, calling himself Carole and breast-feeding a rag doll.

I still keep my clothes in a drawer repaired by the Cambridge Rapist, signed in chalk on the side-panel. Well, he did a lovely job on it.

Flora Hinton

Robert Frost

IT WAS THE winter of 1954. I was a National Serviceman, crossing London towards Waterloo for the train back to a bleak barrack-room at Aldershot. With a little time to spare I made for the National Gallery to spend a few minutes with Jan Arnolfini and his wife. I felt I needed something to lift my gloom before being dragged back into a world of parade grounds, shouting corporals and Blanco.

Near the steps an elderly man approached me. 'I need some help,' he said. 'I've got to make a phone call and I don't seem to know how to use your telephones.' He was thin and a little dishevelled and had an American accent. 'Come with me and we'll find a box,' I said. As we walked across Trafalgar Square he explained that he had just arrived in London and wanted to contact a friend with whom he would be staying. 'I've come over to see my publisher about an English edition of my verse,' he volunteered. From a bulging briefcase he produced a book which he handed to me. 'This is how it came out in the States,' he said.

On the cover I saw the name, ROBERT FROST. Opening it, the frontispiece was a portrait of him by Wyndham Lewis. I think I said something inane like 'Wow!'

We found a phone box, and after some searching he unfolded a scrap of paper with the number he wanted me to dial. 'Familiar with Picasso?'

he asked suddenly.

'Of course,' I replied. Until the previous July I had been an art student.

'I was with him a few days ago,' he said. 'As I was leaving I was looking round his studio and picked up this. He just gave it to me. I've got it here.' He struggled with his briefcase again and handed me a little ink and wax drawing of a bunch of anemones in a jar. I held it disbelievingly, but it was signed 'Picasso'. He returned it to his briefcase, I dialled his number, he nodded his thanks, and I went for my train to the barrack-room in Aldershot.

David Barlow

Oliver Hardy

I KNEW Oliver Hardy for all of five minutes, and never met a kinder or more courteous man, despite the fact that I'd walked in on him unannounced after a long and tiring performance in which he and Stan Laurel, old troupers at the end of their careers, had worked their hearts out in a small provincial theatre. Although I was a young newspaperman at the time, I had no thought of an interview; I just wanted to meet an immortal.

In the mid-'50s, when Laurel and Hardy made their last British tour, they were the penultimate act on a variety bill at Her Majesty's, Carlisle. They were old men now, supposedly past it, and the audience was prepared to be critical. 'They reckon Laurel an' 'Ardy spoil this show,' a red-faced man told the Gents', with grim Cumbrian satisfaction; fifteen minutes later I watched him doubled up and apoplectic with laughter as the two great men appeared from opposite wings and performed that brilliant routine in which neither sees the other, turning in bewilderment behind each other's backs with a speed and perfection of timing that would have graced a ballet.

On an impulse I went backstage during the last act. There were two doors labelled 'Stan Laurel' and 'Oliver Hardy'. I chose Hardy's without hesitation, knocked, heard the well-known voice call 'Come in!', and there he was, sitting four-square, bowler on head, hands on knees, wearing that familiar look of weary resignation. I apologised for intruding, and he smiled and waved me to a seat.

'I just wanted to say thank you, Mr Hardy, for everything,' I said, fairly lamely, and he said: 'You're Scottish,' adding that so was he, by descent (and years later I thought of him when I heard Steve McQueen, with precisely the same tilt of the head and quiet satisfaction, announce: 'I'm Scotch.')

Having got in, I was in haste to get out again, for he looked tired, and I'd no wish to be a nuisance, but he reminisced amiably about 'Bonnie Scotland' and 'Putting Pants on Philip', and the happy memories he and 'Stanley' had of Edinburgh and Glasgow.

At last I got up, and thanked him again. 'Thank you,' he said. 'Good of you to drop in. God bless.' We shook hands, and as I reached the door he said 'Hey' softly, and I looked back. He was sitting there, beaming, in the bowler and the baggy suit, and I realised he was giving me the Hardy farewell that all the world remembers: flapping his tie at me with his fingers.

George MacDonald Fraser

Laurens van der Post

IN 1958 I was teaching at a mixed boarding school on the Ammersee in Bavaria and was sent into Munich one morning to collect the lecturer for the school's weekly sixth-form talk. He was staying at the Bayerischer Hof, even in those days a hotel of extraordinary luxury. The lecturer was Laurens van der Post.

He came down the thickly carpeted stairs, past a gigantic display of flowers, and seemed to me to be more expensively dressed than anyone I had ever seen. He was wearing a beautifully made pale grey flannel suit, a silk tie, what I imagined were hand-made brown shoes, and he was carrying a small brown felt hat. Altogether he was small, neat and spruce, his sparse hair combed across the top of his sun-tanned bald head, but there was a suppressed extravagance about him, like an actor playing a small duke.

He spent about 20 minutes talking to local reporters, then I introduced myself and took him to the car, driven by the school driver. On the 30-minute trip back to Schondorf he talked a great deal.

I was sufficiently impressed to put down what he had said in my next weekly letter home, though until then I had never heard of him. He was, I told my parents, 'a fantastically interesting man, and quite charming'.

He said his first language had been Zulu, his second Afrikaans, that he had captained his school hockey team and led their first hunger-strike.

Some of his fellow-pupils had beards, and one was married. At the age of 19, he had captained the South African hockey team, and soon afterwards set sail for England and learned to speak English for the first time.

On his first visit he became friends with Stephen Spender, Graham Greene, Benjamin Britten and Rose Macaulay. Questioned later by our headmaster, he admitted that he did not know the Queen herself, but he was a close friend of the Queen Mother, and from his conversations with her had formed a 'very good impression of the Queen's character'.

Back in South Africa, he founded the magazine *Whiplash* with Roy Campbell, in which he openly attacked Apartheid: it was closed down when Roy Campbell had a row with their backer. Van der Post told many stories about Roy Campbell, in one of which Campbell tried to murder Epstein in a fight over a woman, and the sculptor's wife subsequently dropped one of her husband's works on Campbell's head as he passed beneath her window.

Van der Post had then, he told me, travelled to Japan, and become fluent in the language. This had stood him in good stead at the outbreak of the Second World War, as he recounts in his book *A Bar of Shadow*, when he was parachuted behind the Japanese lines in Java.

There, he told us, 'without any supplies or radio communication', he had carried on a guerilla war against the Japanese 'in the company of a Swiss geologist and a beautiful Javanese princess'. Deserted by his doctor, he was visiting the sick one morning when he found himself surrounded by a Japanese patrol, who charged at him with fixed bayonets. Only his request to them in faultless formal Japanese to 'wait an honourable minute' had stopped them. At the end of the war he acted as negotiator between the Javanese rebels and the Dutch, and remembered being present as 'the only white man in a crowd of 20,000 yellow men' as an old Javanese rebel returning from Russia had begged them with tears in his eyes never to have anything to do with the Russians, 'who stole one's heart and one's mind'.

His talk to the school concentrated mainly on the Kalahari, about which he told what even I in my innocence described to my parents as 'fantastic stories'. Witch doctors consulted invisible crowds, machinery jammed on sacred mountains, and he himself had paddled through swamps in a bark canoe when two giant crocodiles rose from the water only feet away, locked in a death-struggle.

I think what I remember most clearly, but did not include in my letter home, is the way his eyes flashed when he told the children about his prowess as a hunter. When he was in London, he said, he was always finding shillings and half-crowns lying on the pavement, being trained and alert to the threat of snakes on the jungle paths. Before he left, we walked down through the village, and he raised his brown hat in greeting to the lake. In Africa, he said, it was the custom to raise your hat to the Great Spirit of the Water.

John Wells

Laurence Olivier

IN 1977 MY FRIEND Richard Stroud offered me the part of Socrates in *The Gadfly*, a film about that lay saint's trial and death he was making for Granada. I stayed at the Midland, Manchester's grandest hotel.

Although things had gone fairly well during the walk-throughs, on the morning of the first day's filming I went down to breakfast frightened, timid, certain that I would forget my part, depressed at what my fame-seeking vanity had got me into. The breakfast-room was full. Everyone else looking forward to the day's work, I told myself. Then, sitting at a table near to the centre of that large room I saw Sir Laurence, who – thanks to Lady Olivier (Joan Plowright), a friend from the late Fifties – I knew slightly. Looking up, he saw and remembered me.

I explained what I was doing in Manchester. Then, to my own surprise, I blurted out: 'I am scared stiff. I don't know what to do. I shall let every-one down.'

Without a moment's hesitation he stood up, put his arms under my arms, lifted me off the floor and shook me, hard, saying: 'Nonsense, you will be fine. Fine.'

Then he put me down and went back to his kipper. No one had paid the slightest attention. I felt really good, ate a big breakfast, and went to the studios determined to do my best.

Christopher Logue

Artur Schnabel

SOME TIME in the mid-Thirties, probably in the autumn of 1935, Artur Schnabel and Bronislaw Huberman came to the City Hall in Sheffield to give a recital of violin sonatas by Mozart, Beethoven and Brahms.

During my student days I had played most of the sonatas of these composers with my college tutor and so, fortunately as things turned out, I happened to be familiar with the three that Schnabel and Huberman had chosen to play: Mozart in E flat, K 380; Beethoven in C minor, Op 30 No 2; and Brahms in G, Op 78.

On the day of the concert I arrived early, anxious to find a good seat and enjoy the atmosphere in the hall before the start of the music. I had barely settled down in my seat and was beginning to read the programme when an official tapped me on the shoulder and asked me if I would kindly step outside for a moment. Wondering what on earth I had done wrong, I was taken aback when he asked me if I would be good enough to turn over the music for the two performers.

I was nervous and flustered. Why had this gentleman picked on me, and how did he know that I could read music? However, there was no time for questions. Before I knew what was happening I was being whisked downstairs to the artistes' room to be introduced to the two great men. Schnabel had long been one of my heroes. I was thrilled to meet him, but full of trepidation about what lay ahead.

With Teutonic thoroughness Schnabel began to introduce me to the gentle art of the 'turner-overer'. First my chair. It had to be placed at just the right distance from the piano: close enough for me to see the music comfortably, but not so close that I might hamper the pianist's movements. I then had to learn how to settle down on the chair, adopting a decent posture, and how to rise slowly and gracefully when the time came to move across to the piano and turn over a page of music. These movements were rehearsed a number of times.

Artur Schnabel used a chair in performance and not a piano stool. He kept quite still, no histrionics or exaggerated movements, although, like Glenn Gould, he did occasionally sing tonelessly and grunt a little when he was particularly moved by the power of the music. (In his attitude at the keyboard he reminded me of Rachmaninov, whom I had also heard play in the same hall. Rachmaninov too sat very still with his back as straight as a Guardsman's, his striking Slavonic features revealing no emotion as the most ravishing sounds came out of the piano.)

We next turned our attention to the printed pages. On each RH page of the pianist's music were red and blue pencil marks and occasionally a green one. A red mark was a signal for me to rise slowly from my chair and move across to the piano, ready to turn over the page when the music reached the blue mark. I had to turn the page gently, holding the top RH corner. 'No dog ears,' growled Schnabel. When a green mark appeared I had to walk across to the violinist's music stand – very slowly, of course – and turn over his page. All this was rehearsed.

I think this careful attention to detail increased rather than diminished my nervousness. When the steward appeared to summon us to the concert platform I must have looked a little tense and apprehensive. As we mounted the steps that led to the platform Artur Schnabel gave me a beaming smile and patted me on the back in fatherly fashion.

'Do not worry,' he whispered. 'We know it all by heart.'

Edwin Smith

RS Thomas

DECISIONS, in retrospect, are often impossible to explain. For instance, why did my normally sensible friend, John Bolton, Head of English at Coalbrookedale High School, decide to hold a poetry speaking competition in the spring of 1957? And why did the already distinguished poet (and reclusive vicar of a remote mid-Wales parish), RS Thomas, consent to adjudicate the event? But these events did occur – although, in the context, 'collided' might be a more apposite verb.

The great man arrived in good time to enjoy a dinner with the Headmaster, served in the privacy of his study. The Head was a good-natured, sociable man who had gladly entered into the spirit of the occasion so it was surprising, to say the least, when, a mere 15 minutes later, his worried face came round the door of the men's staff room saying, 'Take him off my hands, John, for God's sake, I don't know what to do with him!'

There was still half an hour before afternoon school. What could be done but show the honoured guest into the staff room, which was quickly vacated by all those who thought the event was a waste of time anyway. The art teacher, also an affable man and himself a published poet, was introduced but fared no better than the Head in getting more than minimal response to any conversational endeavour. Even the spring sunshine coming through the window could do nothing to lighten the leaden gloom of

Thomas's aura.

In desperation, the afternoon bell was rung early and the school filed into the assembly hall. Girls far outnumbered boys in entering the competition – sensitive, imaginative girls almost by definition, and something of Thomas's reputation already filled them with awe and apprehension. One entrant withdrew, physically sick, though fortunately not publicly so. The programme made its nervous progress and finally Thomas was asked to nominate the winners. I don't think anyone disagreed with his choices but many were amazed when he began his overall adjudication by saying, 'I don't know why I have come here today, because I think poetry should never be read aloud.'

The Head invited the sixth form and any other staff or pupils who wished to take advantage of our distinguished guest to join a discussion in the library. Thomas said he had nothing to add to his previous homily but consented to answer questions. A mischievous member of staff asked, 'If, despite your disapproval of reading poetry aloud, you were nevertheless placed in a situation where you had to do so, could you please show us how it should be done?' Everyone held their breath. Thomas sighed, 'Have you a copy of Hopkins?'

John Bolton whisked a volume of Gerard Manley Hopkins' works from a shelf and Thomas began –

Margaret, are you grieving
Over Goldengrove unleaving?

as if reading the funeral litany over a dearly-loved parishioner. Stifled sniffling began among several sixth form girls, and by the time he reached

And yet you will weep and know why

audible sobbing had half the audience in its grasp.

The ritual parting cup of tea was foregone. We watched his departure from the staff room window as his little Austin A30 van rolled down the long ramp to the school gate. Before turning into the road he paused, looked back, raised his hand and, for the first time, smiled.

Arthur Arnold

Arnold Bax

IN THE EARLY 1930s, when I was Organ Scholar at Keble College, Oxford, one of the dons, A S Owen – known as 'The Crab' – used to take a handful of undergraduates to the annual Three Choirs Festival. The year I was included, the venue was Gloucester.

The Crab expected us to attend the daytime concerts in the cathedral, but in the evenings we could do as we liked. The more conscientious would go to chamber music recitals at the Shire Hall.

One very hot evening as I stood outside that hall, strongly tempted to cut the concert as I was allergic to stuffy, BO-ridden halls, I noticed a much older man standing opposite me and looking very ill-at-ease. With the audience all in and the doors about to shut, I called out to him: 'Aren't you going in? I believe they are doing some Arnold Bax.' 'I am Arnold Bax,' he replied, and before I had had time to recover from the shock, he said, 'I'm afraid to go in. Why don't we go off and find a nice pub?'

I can't remember how far we walked in the late summer heat, but we certainly went outside the city and off the beaten track.

Bax insisted on paying for all the drinks, which was lucky because I had only a few bob on me. He told me about the claustrophobia he suffered in concert halls and how panic would seize him. He could only go to a concert if he sat close to an exit. When I told him I had waited outside the Shire Hall for somewhat similar reasons, Bax seemed delighted that a stripling should understand the feeling.

As we chatted away, I noticed that he had drunk a great deal more than me. When it was time to go, he had to ask me to help him find his hotel. 'I know its name but I've forgotten where it is.' Luckily, I knew Gloucester well and felt honoured to act as escort to my distinguished friend.

Alas, I never met him again.

Joseph Cooper

Danny Kaye

IT WAS IN 1955 or 1956, in Nigeria. UNICEF, the semi-official children's agency which had been set up after the war, was planning to make a film to draw attention to sick children in Africa, and they had brought in Danny Kaye to take part. Presumably they chose Nigeria because civilised amenities such as hotels, phones, etc, were available, yet Africa in the raw was still easily accessible. I was on the staff of the World Health Organisation in Kano, which was to be the film-maker's first stop, and was asked to liaise with the local authorities.

An ancient walled city, Kano lies not in the tropical south of the country but almost on the edge of the Sahara, and is a thoroughly Moslem town. I remember it as a spread of small, white-washed, one-storey houses thickly scattered along a confusion of narrow dirt lanes, with the twin minarets of the mosque towering over all.

I don't suppose that the Kano scene, though picturesque enough, was what the director of the film had in mind for a film about suffering African children. The local medical people dearly wanted to oblige, but they had little to suggest except their hospital. They were proud of it and only too keen to show it off. The matron was particularly proud of the nurses. They were missionary-educated girls from the south, Christians, capable and dedicated and with a cheerfulness that enabled them to survive in this alien, anti-woman society.

It's unlikely that any of them had even heard of Danny Kaye, let alone seen him on film, but everybody agreed that they deserved the reward of seeing the great film star, perhaps even of appearing in a film. It was suggested that the film team, and Danny, might first visit the local hospital and take a look in the children's ward. It was not a filming session, just a preliminary look round to get the feel of things.

The ward had been tidied up, the grannies who usually slept on the floor under the beds had been shooed out, and the nurses were all lined up in their best uniforms, their shining black faces wreathed in shy grins. The long rows of beds and cots were full of sick children, many of them very ill indeed. Everyone knew that a VIP was going to visit the ward and there was an air of silent expectancy. Even the babies stopped crying for once.

On or off screen, Danny Kaye believed that his mission in life was to make children laugh, and as an old trouper he was determined to make his entrance as dramatic as possible. The doors were flung open and he pranced in, waving his hands, 'Da-de-da, da-de-da', a big smile on his face, an overgrown Pan or Puck. The words faltered, half-out of his mouth, as he took in the scene and realised that his levity was not really appropriate. Trying hard to smile, he looked around. Sitting up in the bed at his side was a little girl, perhaps three or four years old, wondering what was going on. Slowly she turned and looked up at him with big sad eyes. One side of her face was perfectly normal, even pretty, but on the other side, where her cheek had been, was a dark cavernous hole. The lips had gone and a string of glistening white teeth stretched conspicuously across the black hole that was her mouth, surrounded by ulcerous rotting flesh. Known as gangosa or chancrum oris, her condition was common in those days and perhaps is still, where malnutrition and neglect prevail. It was a disturbing enough sight for anyone.

Danny Kaye froze in his tracks, the words jammed in his mouth as he tried hard to retain his agonised grin. His complexion went white, then green. He slumped and turned, gasping for support. 'My God. Take me out of here.' We complied. That was the last I saw of Danny Kaye. I don't know whether they ever made the film.

Bill Norman-Taylor

Jacques Tati

IN THE EARLY SIXTIES I was involved in starting an advertising agency, which, at the time, hadn't become such a commonplace event. To our surprise, we were appointed by one of the major high-street banks. My particular responsibility was writing and producing film commercials, and, as our new client had lagged behind in this sector, I was anxious to impress both him and the advertising industry at large by suggesting that Jacques Tati be invited to make one for us. The script I had concocted for the allegedly more caring bank made its point via Tati's well-known antipathy to automation with a neat little common-man-versus-the-computer plot.

My idea was accepted and I was despatched to Paris to engage the great man, who suggested a number of improvements on the basic idea. He then took me into a cutting-room and showed me a rough version of his forthcoming film, *Traffic*, as he was concerned about a sequence at a petrol station and a joke about a motorist – overloaded with free gifts. He asked me how this could be improved and, keen to respond to the maestro, I said it might be funnier if the gift were more incongruous, say a small bust of Beethoven. Tati fixed me with a cold look and we returned to his office to discuss his fee for the commercial and the logistics of filming it.

As he was about to leave, he suddenly asked 'What about casting?' This came as a nasty shock as my idea depended on the use of his Monsieur

Hulot character, complete with hat, pipe, burberry and umbrella (the fee I had agreed also reflected this, I felt). Tati was adamant. M. Hulot wasn't on the menu. It would not be difficult to find an English actor he could bend to his will. For the rest of the participants, he always relied on real people. The employees of the bank would be ideal.

I returned to London dreading the next meeting with the client. I reported that it was all systems go: Tati was crazy about the idea, but there was a snag – he wouldn't actually figure in the commercial, just direct it. I shut my eyes and waited for blows to rain down on me. 'Thank goodness for that,' I heard the client say: 'We didn't like to say that we felt M. Hulot was a little old for our target audience.'

A branch of the bank was soon chosen for its charm and negotiations were completed for its staff to come in over the weekend to appear in the film. Tati asked to be booked into a simple little pub, whose name he could never pronounce, which turned out to be the Connaught. Shortly after filming started, a worried assistant director told me that Tati would like a word. 'Do you 'ave a black book?' asked the maestro. 'You know, phone numbers of actresses, models, mistresses, etc?' I spent the rest of the day on the telephone trying to rustle up talent.

The film turned out better than I expected and Tati disappeared from my life. Shortly afterwards, I received two tickets for the premiere of *Traffic*. In the middle of the film was quite a funny scene at a petrol station with a motorist's glove compartment crammed with little busts of Beethoven.

Jonathan Abbott

Graham Greene

DURING THE early 1970s, quite soon after my wife achieved her ambition of owning a second-hand bookshop, she took maternity leave. I temporarily gave up the life of a travelling jazz musician to look after the enterprise (in London WC1). Customers were few and far between. In a way this was fortunate because the premises were so tiny that any more than three browsers at a time and the place was packed.

The dimensions made it impossible not to be aware of a customer entering the shop. Usually I looked up from whatever I was reading and attempted a smile, but on this particular morning I was so engrossed in a book-trade magazine that I didn't even glance at the newcomer. The article which so intrigued me was by a bookseller who described a frosty encounter he'd had with Graham Greene. I finished the piece and glanced at my solitary visitor. It was Graham Greene.

I stared disbelievingly at the tall figure and let out an involuntary grunt of amazement. This caused a pair of watery but vividly blue eyes to focus on me in a way that seemed to demand an explanation for the ugly sound.

'You won't believe this, Mr Greene, but I was just reading an account of you visiting a small second-hand bookshop and I look up and here you are.'

He gave a rather wan smile as I backed up my story by waving the magazine at him.

'Yes, I've read that, but naturally I viewed the incident rather differently.'

I was completely nonplussed. The publication had only arrived that morning. Was the great man's reading list so extensive that he'd already found time to take in the contents of a small-circulation trade journal? Apparently so, because he went on to give his own amusing description of his visit to the bookshop.

He talked about living in Bloomsbury years before. He didn't visit the area often but was doing so in order to see a friend who was a patient in the nearby Italian hospital. He spotted a book, *Where Black Rules White*, and this led him on to discussing Haiti. I mentioned Haitian music and he gave a marvellous account of being kept awake by a band on the outskirts of Port-au-Prince.

I wanted to make a gift of the book he'd chosen, *Ezra Pound in Kensington*, but he insisted on paying for it. I pulled a copy of *Our Man in Havana* from a shelf and asked if he'd mind signing it. He asked my name and wrote a warm inscription. I thanked him and mentioned film criticism, which led him to reeling off a string of yesteryear stars, including Harold Lloyd. I commented that Lloyd had named one of his characters Harold Diddlebock only to find that real Mr H D had jumped up and demanded an apology. Greene smiled and said 'I always make a special point of avoiding any name that might be recognised.'

We shook hands and he buttoned his excessively long black overcoat and left. Some while later I read Greene's novel *The Human Factor* and saw that the author had named a character (who appears once) Chilton.

John Chilton

Harold Macmillan

IN MAY 1981, aged 22, I went to stay at Birch Grove, the Macmillan family home. I was an usher at a wedding where Harold Macmillan's grandson David was best man. I knew Macmillan himself lived in the house but his status was unclear. From what I had gathered, there was an element of *King Lear* about it, the Grand Old Man having given up his crown and his retinue.

The wedding had been in the afternoon and after the reception I was late getting to Birch Grove, with just enough time for a bath before going out to dinner and dancing. By the time I found my bedroom, bathroom and cold bathwater I was later still. Everybody else had left as I ran down the stairs tying my black tie.

As I passed the drawing-room, I glanced in. Macmillan was sitting upright in an armchair, tapping a stick on the carpet.

'Good evening, sir,' I said, still moving swiftly.

'Young man, come in here.' I stopped. Poor old boy, I thought, all alone and starved of conversation. But I had other business.

'Sir, I'm rather late for the party after the wedding – you know, where your grandson was best man.'

The tapping continued. 'Young man, come in here.'

I stepped over the threshold.

'Young man, there is a mouse running about this room.'

I looked around. He was correct. A mouse had found its way into the house and was trying to get out again.

'Yes, sir,' I said, 'It's a field mouse. Shall I leave the door open for it?'

'Young man, I want you to kill that mouse.'

'But sir, it's only trying to get out.'

'Young man, you are not going to your party until you have killed that mouse.'

Aged 22, I thought I knew no fear. But I was wrong. Motionless apart from the tapping of the stick, Macmillan watched me from under those heavy lids with dispassion. I only existed to remove the inconvenience that scurried from corner to corner, curious and afraid. Was I a man or a mouse? I was a mouse.

Leaning against the fireplace was a cast-iron coal shovel. I picked it up. My first two attempts were unsuccessful but the mouse did not seem to understand the danger. On the third attempt, I hit it cleanly on the head. Death was at least quick. I swept the mouse up on the shovel and presented it to Macmillan.

'Young man, you may now go to your party.'

I left the room with a shovel and mouse, went outside and threw the corpse into a hedge. I went back inside to replace the shovel.

Macmillan ignored me. But the tapping had stopped.

Napier Miles

Sir Alec Guinness

THE OCCASION was a sale by auction of rare books – mostly modern first editions and private press volumes – at Sotheby's popular Chancery Lane rooms, in the late 1970s.

I was officiating at the desk beside the rostrum, and after about 30 years' experience in the book trade, I knew – at least by name or face – quite nine-tenths of the 'groundlings' sitting or standing below me. Not so the auctioneer who was conducting the sale. A private press edition of one of Shakespeare's plays came up for sale. I can't remember which one it was now. As I recall it was a handsomely printed tome, bound in green.

Bidding was brisk, and I noticed, in the far left-hand corner of the room, that one of the competitors was a rather ordinary-looking gentleman, very soberly dressed in a dark blue overcoat.

Being something of a film buff, I caught on to those features immediately, and I watched with interest as the bidding went back and forth. Finally, down came the hammer with a bang, and at a very respectable price. But to my amazement, the auctioneer called one of the well-known London booksellers as the purchaser! I never saw a face drop so far as that of that 'ordinary' punter at the far end of the room. And it was here that I stepped in.

'Oh,' I said to the auctioneer, 'Sir Alec was bidding.'

If I'd said that Alf Bloggs had been bidding, I doubt if it would have made much difference. But the title I mentioned had made a great deal. The lot was put up again, but the dealer had reached his limit. The Shakespeare went to the chap in the far corner.

'Sir Alec Guinness,' I called loudly, since nobody else, including the man selling, seemed to be aware of who the buyer was. Naturally, there was a muttering, and a slight turning of heads, but I then forgot all about it and concentrated on the many lots to come before this auction was over.

Some short while later, a modest figure put in a quiet appearance beside me at the desk. Sir Alec nodded gratefully, and thanked me for intervening on his behalf.

He paid me for his purchase, which he was obviously very happy to have made, I receipted his bill, he collected the book from the porter, and departed – blue overcoat, black bowler hat, *et al*.

O F Snelling

John Christie

I COULD EASILY have ended my life as a body hidden under the floor-boards at Ten Rillington Place. In 1940 I was doing shuttle service outside the War Office in Whitehall. I was in the ATS. It was a cold day, pouring with rain, when a policeman tapped on my car window. He said, 'Come and have a coffee in the block-house, there are other War Office staff there.'

I didn't want a coffee, but the FANYs had a reputation for being snooty, so I agreed. He said he'd go on and for me to follow. I locked the car and ran back the 100 yards to the blockhouse. I entered a small low aperture, surrounded by sandbags, and found myself in a narrow passage. I walked to the end and heard a sound. I turned and saw him standing in the entrance, his eyes staring.

I said, 'I came in here for a coffee and nothing else. If you put a finger on me, I'll give such a scream I'll bring the whole War Office out. I have many influential friends.' I hadn't a soul, in fact.

He didn't speak again but dived at me, knocking me back against the wall at the end of the passage where there was an orange crate. Then he grabbed my throat with one hand and pinched my nose with the other so that I couldn't breathe. With all my strength I kicked him in the crotch with my army issue shoe. He staggered back and I dived for the entrance.

My heart beating like a sledge-hammer, I rushed back to my car and drove off at high speed.

That night I rang my father. 'What shall I do? I was attacked by a policeman.'

My father, full of concern, asked, 'Did he hurt you? Did he touch you? Did you get his number?'

I said I was unhurt; it had been raining, and his cape had covered his number.

'Forget it then, do nothing. Who would believe the word of an ATS girl against that of a policeman?' was my father's advice.

So I forgot it, but I knew that I would never be able to forget those eyes. The war ended, I got married and had three sons. Then one morning in 1953 I opened the newspaper – and there were those same eyes staring up at me. I screamed for my husband. 'That's the man who attacked me,' I said and pointed to the hateful face.

'Nonsense,' he replied.

'Look in the paper and see if he has ever been a policeman.' I knew I was right.

There were five pages about his awful crimes, with horrific details of all the women who had been strangled. Eventually he looked up. 'My God, he was a Special Constable in the War Reserve Police in 1940.'

He rang 999 and in seconds was put through to Sir Lionel Heald, who was leading for the Crown. Sir Lionel asked my husband if I had children. He told him that we had three little boys and that we lived in the country. Sir Lionel said, 'Give me your name and address – but I don't want to call your wife. It is the most appalling case and we have enough evidence to hang Christie a hundred times.'

And so he was – at Pentonville that same year, on 15 July.

I'm 81 now. Last month I saw in the paper that there was to be a repeat of the film *Ten Rillington Place*. My blood ran cold.

Judy Cameron-Wilson

Enoch Powell

ENOCH POWELL wasn't much of a customer. His wife was the one who spent the money, regularly buying kitchen utensils and garden tools from my father's ironmongers shop in Wolverhampton's Chapel Ash.

During its final years the shop's trade had declined and my father ran the place alone. From time to time he'd ask me to take over so that he could enjoy a much needed weekend break. It was towards the end of a dismal November day and I was looking forward to closing up and heading homewards. There had been no customers since half past five and, as I began to cash up at ten to six, rain was falling steadily in the darkness outside. There were rarely any customers during the last half-hour of the day and I often wondered why my father never chose to close the shop that much earlier. It was only years after that I realised the shop's closing time coincided with the opening of The Clarendon, the congenial pub only a step away, where Dad invariably put a full stop to the day's business.

I was locking the back door when the phone rang. I picked up the receiver and heard the unmistakable tones of Enoch Powell. He had a curious accent – what I can only describe as 'posh Wolverhampton'.

'Don't close yet,' he ordered me. 'I'll be there in five minutes.'

I was very young and he was a distinguished statesman, so I did as I was told. All the same, by five past six I decided he wasn't coming after all, so I switched off the lights and made for the front door, which I'd locked while counting the day's takings. As I reached it there was a loud tapping on the glass. The prominent eyes of Enoch Powell peered from his pale face into the gloom within. His moustache quivered with urgency and water streamed from the broad rim of his black Homburg hat. Reluctantly I let him in and locked the door behind him, wondering what problem was so urgent it was worth braving such foul weather. He marched up to the counter, pulled a green-stained brass garden tap from the pocket of his heavy overcoat and placed it in front of me. 'It needs a new washer,' he said, flatly.

I turned on the lights again and asked him what sort of washer it needed. He didn't know; he couldn't get the thing apart. Great, I thought. After several minutes of futile struggle, engaged in a sort of arm-wrestling match with Mr Powell, who held the tap in the grip of a large wrench while I heaved on an equally large spanner, I gave up. 'It's not going to shift,' I said. 'You'd be better off with a new tap.' Enoch Powell, however, gave up less easily.

'We need a vice,' he said. 'You must have one in here somewhere.'

I should have replied with a categorical 'No'. Unfortunately, I hesitated. 'Not really... There's a very old thing upstairs, but...'

He jumped on this eagerly. I explained that there was no light on the top floor; electricity had never been installed beyond the first flight of stairs. In fact, the upper storey of the house was now used only for the storage of unwanted clutter; piles of dusty hessian sacks in which lawn seed had been delivered, broken and unrepaired tools long forgotten and unclaimed by their owners, and several life-sized cardboard figures bearing cheerful smiles as they demonstrated some new product or other. Many years ago, the front room of the top floor had been a simple workshop. The bench my grandfather once used was still there but it now leaned awkwardly at a sharp angle since one of its legs had become detached. The vice was completely rusted over but eventually I managed to open its jaws and, while Enoch held the torch, I tightened them on the resisting tap. Slowly I prised it apart. I picked up the pieces and, taking the torch from Enoch's hand, led the return to the ground floor, periodically shedding the light behind me. It wasn't so much courtesy as a desire not to be crushed to death by a falling Enoch Powell.

Behind the counter, on a high shelf reached only by the small wooden ladder kept for the purpose, was a box of leather washers. I climbed up and brought it down. Inside, the box was partitioned by interlocking cardboard dividers into 24 small compartments, each containing a different size or shape of washer. On the underside of the lid was a diagram replicating its contents with a brief description of each item – three-quarter-inch cup, half-inch heavy duty, etc. Unfortunately, the compartment that should have contained washers of the sort needed was empty. Somehow, I wasn't surprised.

Mr Powell reached into the box and picked out one of the three-quarter-inch cup washers. 'This should do it,' he said. 'It just needs trimming to shape.'

So, naturally, that's what I did. I took up a Stanley knife and trimmed the cup-shaped flange until I'd achieved a three-quarter-inch flat washer – more or less.

I squeezed it into the tap, reassembled the various bits and handed the product of half an hour's labour to what I assumed to be a highly satisfied customer.

'How much do I owe you?' he asked.

I peered at the lid of the box where prices had been written in pencil, probably by my grandfather 25 years earlier.

It read '6d' – six pence in old money.

I should have said six shillings but I was anticipating a handsome tip.

'Sixpence,' I replied.

And that's what he gave me – sixpence – not a penny more.

By the time Enoch Powell had departed into the night, it was turned half past six. I switched off the lights once more, stepped into the still pouring rain, locked the shop door and walked, very briskly, to the pub.

David Thomas